MW01503798

Baseball

'An introduction to the game'

Patrick Lynn

Copyright © 2024 Patrick Lynn

All rights reserved. No part of this publication may be reproduced, distributed, or transmitted in any form or by any means without the prior written permission of the author.

ISBN:

DEDICATION

This book is dedicated to my wife, Jolanta Lynn, and my two boys, Daniel Lynn and Brandon Lynn.

My wife, Jolanta, for having the patience and understanding that the game of baseball requires a lot of work and time away from the family. For always having clean uniforms ready for the boys to wear at each and every game and for the endless support, she has given throughout their journeys.

My boys, Brandon and Daniel, for being the respectful, hardworking young men they have become. For the years of dedication and hard work with both school and baseball. The years of enjoyment, pride, and memories they have brought to my wife and me are priceless. I wish them nothing but success in this world. We will always be by your side with anything you decide to do.

ACKNOWLEDGEMENTS

Special thanks to my wife, Jolanta Lynn, and my two boys, Brandon and Daniel.

Thanks to my parents, James, and Bridget Lynn

My siblings – Kathy, Nuala, Bridget, Maggie, Jimmy, John, and Billy

I'd also like to mention a sincere thanks to.

- My personal proofreader - Brigid Ahern
- All my friends in life, baseball, and my career.
- All the New Hyde Park baseball dads and coaches – "We had a good run."
- The Bethpage "fantastic four" coaches – Coach John, Coach Mike, Coach Bill, and Coach Joey.
- Coach Pat Madigan – you brought out the best in my son.
- Oil City Bandits - Reid and Ryan Gorecki, Fieldhouse – Rick Garrett. Famous Swing Danny Lackner, Prospect Sports – Bobby DeMichael
- "The 'Dads" Jason, Howie, Vinny, Tommy, John (JCI) Brian and Dr

  Mike, "the experience was priceless."
- NHP Gladiators - Joe Rotondaro

AUTHOR'S NOTE

My name is Patrick Lynn. I am one of eight children born to James and Bridget Lynn. I was raised in a small town on Long Island, New York where there were a lot of kids our age we had to play with. Without the technology we have today, we all played outdoors and had the best times of our lives. We played many games, but baseball was the number one sport for us.

Later in life I became an HVAC Operating Engineer to follow in my father's footsteps but kept baseball in my life by umpiring and playing softball with my brothers and friends. I started coaching baseball when my two boys were old enough to play, and that's when I discovered how much I love teaching.

In my career, the opportunity came up for me to work in the training department as an instructor and I jumped at it. My passion for teaching continued there as well. I eventually became the Training Director, a position I currently hold. It gave me the chance to help develop the next generation of engineers and instructors.

I decided to write this book as part of my passion for passing on knowledge I have gained through playing, umpiring, and helping my kids develop as people and players. I am hoping it will help others as well.

Contents

CHAPTER 1

HOW I STARTED

In the spring of 2020, the world faced one of the most severe health crises in history. Many of our daily activities came to an abrupt halt. Work, school, sports, and, most importantly, our social interactions with friends and family were all significantly impacted by this pandemic. We were suddenly asked to stay home, which at first for many seemed like a great idea. Who wouldn't want to stay home instead of going to work or school? Yes, it seemed great initially, but it quickly got old.

As a father of two boys who were highly active in sports, I missed going to games and practices with them. We were all forced to take that time and think about what was important in our lives. It was a time to reflect with family and friends. This was much easier with today's technology and social media, of course. Yes, we all missed sports, but it allowed time to practice independently and work on those things they may have needed to work on. One thing it gave me time to do was work on this book. I have always wanted to write a book about baseball and how it relates to life. At the same time, I was hoping it would help kids understand the roles and responsibilities of each position on the baseball field.

A little about me: as I mentioned earlier, I am the father of two boys. Like me, my boys grew up trying all different types of sports.

I grew up a little differently though, as I was one of eight kids. My parents came to America from Ireland, and baseball is not popular in Ireland. Soccer, or as they call it football, was one of the games played in Ireland. Of course, there is rugby, a game called hurling, and golf with all the green grass. My parents didn't know anything about baseball when I was growing up. The first sport I remember playing was soccer, which was the game they knew, so that was the game we played. Thankfully, we lived on a street where all the other kids knew about baseball, and most played for the town teams.

My parents soon signed us up to play on those teams as well. I don't remember a Tee ball team or farms division, so I think I was about eight when I started playing baseball. I continued playing until I turned eighteen. Not only did we play on the town-organized teams, but we also played just for fun on the street almost every day. We were lucky enough to live on a dead-end street, so we didn't have to worry about traffic. I will never forget; however, when a car came down the street, someone yelled "CAR." We used a tennis ball back then, and I will never know how the neighbors didn't run us off the street. There was always a ball bouncing off someone's car or house.

You know how far they can go if you ever hit a tennis ball with a baseball bat. Sure, we played other games like most kids do but my fondest memories are the baseball games. Now, I was no star on the street, but I could hold my own. I wasn't a star on the organized teams either. I mostly played second base and outfield, batted at the bottom of the lineup, and never hit a home run over the fence. I was fast, though. If a ball got past someone I was home long before they caught up to it. Things were much different back then when we only had dads who would volunteer to coach. No paid coaches like you see today. It was truly a town effort to teach kids how to play, and most of us enjoyed the game. Like I said, I was blessed to be able to play baseball until I was eighteen years old, but I also had to work because I was one of eight kids, after all.

My parents worked very hard to make sure we had everything we needed. If we wanted the bigger things in life, such as a car, we had to get a job and work for it. No college scouts knocked on my door since I was just an average baseball player, so playing baseball for me was over. I loved the game so much, and I wanted to still be around it so I thought to myself, I can make money and be around baseball at the same time if I become an umpire.

Being an umpire wasn't as enjoyable as playing the game, but it offered me a unique perspective. It allowed me to understand and enforce the rules of baseball. However, what I found challenging about town baseball was dealing with the parents. OMG, the parents. I learned that all umpires need glasses, which they suggested several times during the game. Unsurprisingly, those taunts came when a call involved their child for some reason. I also figured out where kids learn bad language at young ages. Yeah, their parents.

The bottom line is that umpires are supposed to be perfect and never make mistakes unless they favor your team, so it's okay. Give the umpires a break, especially at the little league level. They do not make much money and don't have instant replay. They are human and make mistakes, and yes some are worse than others. After being in their shoes, I learned to have more respect for them and tried to teach that to my kids.

After a few years of umpiring, I started playing adult softball with my brothers and some friends. That was not as fun for me as baseball had been, but we still had a great time because we were all friends and knew the players on most of the teams we played against. The ball is bigger, and because we played arc ball and not fast pitch, it was easier for us older people to hit a slower-pitched ball. That's when I became a home run hitter. Most fields didn't have fences, so I would usually hit the ball past the outfielder.

Remember, I said I was fast, so that helped. I hit my share of homers over the few fences at the few fields that had them. I still mostly played second base, but I also pitched. I never had the arm to pitch with baseball, but I could manage it because we were throwing slowly and underhand. The fast-pitched softball that many people play today is very tough. The mound is closer to the batter, and players can throw very hard. This book is labeled as a baseball book because that is the game I know most about, but almost everything in here can also apply to softball. Anytime I refer to baseball, you can add softball to that.

I played softball up to the age of about thirty-five and stopped after I got married. We had our two boys, and I couldn't wait to get a glove on their hands and have a catch. They were able to start playing at a younger age than I did, so that was great. My sons are two years apart and started playing when they were six. They began playing Tee ball and worked their way up as they got older. As you'd expect, I signed right up to be a volunteer coach. I was able to coach my older boys' team for a few years and then I actually coached both my boys' teams for a short time. That was tough. I always had the philosophy that I was going to teach my boys as much as I could about the game and take the rest of the team along for the ride. What I mean by that is whatever I was teaching my boys, I wanted to teach every kid on their team.

My sons were in the sixth and eighth grades when I started writing this book. They were done with town baseball and, therefore, with me as their coach. They have both moved on to travel baseball as well as school ball. I could not have been prouder when both boys won their first tournaments of the season on the same day. Currently, both boys are playing above their grade level and are both pitchers. They are much better ballplayers than I was at their age. Neither started out as homerun hitters, but they developed power over time. They both have very good plate discipline and can put the ball in play. They don't swing at bad pitches and can recognize speed changes.

As much as I loved coaching, I have to say that I really enjoy just watching them play now. Of course, I will always work with them on fundamentals and answer any questions they may have but watching them play is so much fun. I hope I'm not one of those annoying parents, but I'm sure I have been at times. Let's face it, some umpires do need glasses!

All kidding aside, being an umpire at the kid level is very tough, especially without instant replay. They see the play in real-time and must make a call. Of course, any close calls are when they get the screaming help from both sides.

In this book, I would like to give my take on baseball based on my experience with playing, coaching, and my time as an umpire to teach kids what I feel they need to know about the game. This book will be more about the mental approach to the game and not so much about mechanics. Their coaches and trainers will manage that.

CHAPTER 2

IT'S A GAME, NOT A JOB

First of all, let's remember that baseball at any level where you are NOT getting paid to play is a game and not a job. A job is something you do to earn money. If parents and coaches push you to work like it's a job and not fun for you, then it's not a game to them. It is no longer fun when winning means more to a coach or parent than how you played the game. The game becomes a chore, and you may feel you must perform well every game, or someone will be disappointed.

Don't get me wrong. I believe and have always been taught that if you want anything in life, you have to work hard for it. The key word there is "want." If you **want** to play, not your coach or even your parents, but if you **want** to play, a parent's job is to show you different paths in life and let you decide based on something you want to do. Now that could go in another direction because of today's technological world that we live in today. Unfortunately, video games have a hold on most kids, and given the choice of working on baseball skills or playing video games, the video games will win most of the time. I heard the term again recently "forcing to be an athlete."

That means when parents force kids to play a sport. Maybe it's a sport they played when they were young and know a lot about.

Whatever the case may be, when someone is forced to do anything in life, it is not fun. Now, I have experienced times when my kids would rather play video games than go to practice. I get it. It's easier and maybe more fun to sit and play a video game than to get up, get dressed, put on all the gear, and go to a field. I also see that once they are on the field, they forget about video games and are having a great time. If I had seen that being on the field practicing or playing a game is torture for them, I would not have made them play. With that said, I would not let them sit and play video games all day, either.

I believe in balance. Yes, they love to play video games, but I also have a rule that they must pick two activities they will do after school and during the summer. I don't care if it doesn't involve sports. It could be chess, or music, or theater. Something that they are interested in besides video games. That is why I said earlier that a parent's job is to show kids different paths.

My two boys started with karate. They tried soccer, lacrosse, wrestling, boxing, MMA, basketball, and baseball. The two sports they seem to enjoy the most are basketball and baseball. They are planning on trying football during the upcoming school year. Who knows, maybe they will love football as well, but maybe not. The bottom line is I will support them no matter what path they choose as long as they are safe. There are many reasons why I am glad they both chose baseball as their main sport. The first reason is that I feel like baseball is similar to life. I am currently the Director of an apprentice program where I was a teacher before that. When I was teaching, I'd tell my students that I could relate any life situation to a baseball situation. You will see that as you read on.

Throughout this book, I will discuss every position on the field and how each should be played on offense and defense. I will talk about the physical and mental aspects of the game. The best part of baseball to me is that it is a true team sport where you need every player to be part of it. You practice together, you play games together, you win together, and you lose together. It is never a single play or player that wins or loses a game. I will explain that more later. There is no other game where you are expected to fail more than succeed. Sounds funny, right? It's true.

You are considered a great player if you are a hitter who gets a thousand at-bats and only gets three hundred hits. That means you got out seven hundred times and you are considered great? Yes, that's how hard this game is. The ability to hit a small round ball with a round bat is extraordinary. Seven hundred outs seem like a lot. I was never concerned with the outs. I was concerned about how you got out. Did you go down swinging? Did you go down looking? Did you hit a shot to the fence and get robbed of a home run? Did you hit a screaming line drive right to a player? Was it a hard-hit ground ball? How you get out means a lot.

The three hundred hits I am talking about is about a .300 batting average and at the major league professional baseball player level, that is amazing. Yes, you will see kids batting .500 or better at younger ages. Trust me, the older you get, the lower your batting average will be. As you will see, every position has a responsibility for every play. As you read on, I will explain each position. One term you will see over and over is "game awareness." I cannot stress game awareness enough. You must always be aware of the game, even while sitting on the bench. I used to love to test my players as a coach.

While kids were sitting on the bench waiting to get in the game, I would surprise them by asking them about the current situation. What inning? How many outs? What's the count? What should a player do if the ball is hit to a certain position? If they couldn't answer they do not have game awareness. I will try to explain that this is a life lesson. If you are not paying attention while sitting on the bench, then how can I put you in to help the team? That may be a situation later in life during your career. If you want a promotion but are not paying attention to how that job is done, how can you expect to be chosen?

If a boss asks you what you would do in a situation and your answer is, "I wasn't paying attention," good luck being considered for the promotion if it comes up. It is the same with not being a starter on the team. If you accept that you are not as good as the starters and don't need to learn the game better, you may never be a starter. Having game awareness means paying attention to every situation as it comes up and not waiting for the ball to be hit to you to decide what to do if it **is** hit to you.

You need to know how many outs there are, how many runners are on base, the pitch count, the inning, the score, and who is at bat. Is it a power hitter? Is it a slap hitter? What have you seen him do in any previous at-bats? Are the runners on base fast? Are they taking big leads? Wow, that sounds like a lot to be aware of.

There **is** a lot to be aware of at young ages, and kids are not and should not be expected to be mindful of all the factors. They are learning and hopefully being coached on those situations and factors. They must be repeatedly reminded to be ready and think about what they will do with the ball if it is hit to them. Some coaches will ask kids, "How many times do I have to tell you?" My answer to them is *as many times as it takes*. That's your job as a coach. It is vital to have patience and teach at each player's level of understanding. The players will eventually get it. Maybe not all at the same time, but they will get it. That is why practice is so important.

Demonstrating skills and letting the players see things done is a much better way to learn. Even better is to do something over and over to create what they call muscle memory and have a good baseball IQ. When you reach a good level of baseball awareness , you can better develop your baseball IQ. That's when you will become a **player** at a different level. When you watch the pros play, it is truly remarkable how they make the difficult plays look so easy. It's because they know what they will do with the ball before it is hit.

They also know what to do when it's not hit to them, which leads me to say every player on the field has a job with every at-bat.

Throughout this book, I will be using some baseball terms you probably already know but I'll mention them anyway, like home plate may be called *the dish*.

Coaches tell their players, *"Who's behind the dish!"* for a game. That would be who's catching.

You may hear who is *"on the bump"* for pitchers or the mound, or the *"hill"* or the *"rubber."* All are referring to *the pitcher's mound*. Bases might be called bags. *"In the hole"* might refer to any ball hit between players on the field. That could be a hole in the infield or outfield. You also might hear the same term "in the hole" when someone will be getting up to bat after the player on deck. *"On deck"* is the batter up after the player currently at the plate batting. AB will be referring to *"at bats"* meaning the times you got up to hit.

The diamond refers to the field because of the shape the bases take when connected. Each position in the field has a number.

Number	Position
1	Pitcher
2	Catcher
3	First base
4	Second base
5	Third base
6	Shortstop
7	Left field
8	Center field
9	Right field
DH	Designated hitter *(Does not play in the field)*
PH	Pinch Hitter (*May come into the game to hit in someone's place*)
EH	Extra hitter. *(You will only see this in Little League or travel. Not in high school, college, or pros).*

You may ask why shortstop isn't considered position 5 instead of third base. In the early days of baseball, they used four outfielders. Later, the 6-position moved into where the shortstop plays today. The number just stayed the same.

Before each game, a coach will fill out a lineup card. Copies of this card will typically be given to the other team as well as the umpires. You may give a copy to the tournament director if you are playing in a tournament. The card will list the order in which each player will bat in the lineup as well as their jersey number and the position they will be playing. It will look something like this.

# in order	Jersey #	Name	Position
1	27	Smith	3
Sub			
2	30	Lynch	8
Sub			
3	11	Thomson	1
Sub			

You notice the "Sub" under each position in the lineup. That means a substitute player can come into the game at any time and take that spot in the lineup. This can happen if there is a big roster, and the coach wants to use every player at some point in the game or an injury. Sometimes, it can be an offense or defense strategy.

I could mention many more baseball terms, but I will try and explain them if they come up. Let's get started with the positions.

CHAPTER 3

OUTFIELD

At younger ages, the outfield is usually considered the place where kids who are not that good play. You will see that is not entirely true. It may be true at younger ages but more for safety than skill. Some kids develop different muscles at different times. The muscles I am most concerned about are called the quick twitch muscles, which are responsible for how fast you can react to a hard-hit ball coming right at you. As a coach, if I noticed a kid with a slower reaction time, it would be hard for me to put them in a corner position. The corner positions are first base and third base. The corner positions require faster reaction times because you are positioned closer to the batter, and the ball gets on you faster.

Shortstop and second base allow for more range and more time to react. The pitcher is in the most dangerous position because they are the closest to the batter and not in the best position to field a ball hit back at them after they throw a pitch. Luckily, it does not happen very often. Back to playing the outfield. As you may know, there are three outfield positions. Left field, right field, and center field. As you get older, the three outfield positions require some different skillsets, whereas, for a young player, there is not much difference between the three positions. You will have to earn one of those positions when you get older based on specific abilities. For instance, speed, ability to track a ball and arm strength are all determining factors in deciding which position a player would be best trained to play. Center field requires you to be very fast. You are the help for both right and left fields, so you have the most ground to cover. Your right fielder must have a very strong arm for the more distant plays to third base. Of course, with any long throws, you should be looking for your cutoff man, but that cutoff man can then decide if the throw is on target so they can let it go through or if it is a little off, so they need to cut it off and redirect the throw. It's not that you need to reach; rather, the faster the ball gets to the target, the better. Even if it bounces before reaching the target, it will get there faster without a cut.

So, a strong, accurate arm is important for all three outfield positions but more so for right fielders. Left fielders may get more plays in the outfield due to the abundance of right-handed batters. Left fielders need to be very good in the field and have good baseball IQ. Let's talk about game awareness again. The outfielders need to be aware of the entire situation. *What if the ball gets hit to me? Are there runners on base? Where is the play being called out by the catcher? How far will I have to throw to make a play?* Let's talk about each position as it comes up.

No outs, no one on base. No score. The ball gets hit to right field. It's a hard-hit line drive that bounces once before you field it. At younger ages, you may have a play at first base. Make the throw. Hopefully the catcher is backing up the first baseman on the throw just in case of a bad throw. On the bigger fields, it's a tough play to make. The decision to make that play on the bigger fields should be based on the batter's speed, your arm strength, and accuracy.

Ok, what if it's a routine ground ball hit between first and second base? You have no play at first so your cutoff man should be there set up for a relay to second base. I have always taught my players to follow a simple rule of thumb. You should be planning to throw the ball two bases ahead of where the lead runner is starting from.

For example, no one on base. The batter is the potential lead runner, so two bases ahead of them would be second base. If there is a runner on first, I am throwing the ball two bases ahead to third. If there is a runner on second, I am throwing home. What if the bases are loaded? Where is my throw from the outfield on a ball hit on the ground? You have a small chance of throwing a runner out running from third to home but the runner behind them is starting from second base. That's who I am concerned about. I want to make sure that they are only advancing one base and not able to score. So, my throw is still going home, keeping the ball in front of the runner.

Now, some may be asking, if the runner is starting from second and running to third, why would I make the throw to home and not third? That is because the throw is coming from the outfield, and we are using the 2-base rule of thumb. If you make a bad throw to third on a close play, maybe that runner scores. By throwing the ball home, even if it's a bad throw, the runner shouldn't have enough time to score, especially if there is someone backing up the throw.

Remember, there are situations where you may throw to third. Maybe the ball was hit to left field, which is closer to third, and you may have an easy play. Maybe the ball was hit shallow, and the outfielder fielded the ball while running in. That gives them momentum to make a good throw to third holding the runner at second. Again, baseball situations, just like life situations, are endless. We at least have these rules of thumb to go by. So, in this bases-loaded situation, we may not be able to get the runner out coming from third base, but we certainly want to prevent the runner from second going home as well. The cutoff man can decide to hold the ball going home if they see that the runner from second is not trying to score. They may even have a play at third if the runner is slow or if they go too far while rounding third. So, as a rule of thumb for outfielders, any ball hit on the ground to you should go two bases ahead from where the lead runner is starting.

Once you learn game awareness, you will develop the instincts to make those changing situational plays. Ask some dads and coaches how frustrating it is to watch a kid in the outfield hold on to a ball that was hit to them because they don't know where to throw it. Next thing you know, a single turns into a three-run triple. I tell kids to watch the pros; even on a routine play to the outfield where there is no play, the outfielder and cutoff person still make the throws two bases ahead. We will talk about the job of the cutoff man later.

Ok so we talked about balls hit on the ground right at you. What if the ball is in the gap between the outfielders? Those are tough plays, and I have another rule about that. If a ball gets past the outfielders, it will usually be a double for the batter. That means you should be looking three bases ahead. With no one on base, the throw should be set up for third base. Once again, your cutoff man will be listening to the coach or catcher yell which base to set up for and make the throw. So again, it's just a rule of thumb to have some idea where the play might be.

Now, let's talk about catching a fly ball. One of the most common mistakes an outfielder makes is running in for a fly ball before they see the track that ball is on. Another rule of thumb for fly balls is to take the first step back, NOT in. Even if you eventually realize you must run in to make the catch, by taking that first step back, you can take that split second to better judge the track of the ball. By immediately running in, you risk misjudging the track of the ball, and the next thing you know, the ball is hit over your head.

A routine fly ball becomes a double or triple. The hardest ball to track is the ball hit directly at you in the air. It is much easier to see the track of the ball when it is at an angle. That is why you will sometimes see an outfielder move into a position where there is a slight angle instead of directly at them. They will also set themselves in a position to throw the ball once it is caught by catching the ball while their momentum is moving forward towards the play. I can't stress enough that every player needs to be in a ready position before every pitch is thrown. Since most of the time, an outfielder will be running to a ball that is hit; you must also be ready to get that jump needed to get the ball back in as quickly as possible and hopefully have time to set up for the throw.

Sometimes, outfielders may feel they will have plenty of time to get a ball because the batter is so far away from them. Remember that if a ball is hit hard enough to get into the outfield it is most likely hit harder than the pitcher is throwing. For example, if a pitcher is throwing 60mph and a batter hits a clean line drive into the outfield, that ball could be traveling at 70 mph or more. It will get to you fast.

Some big leaguers are hitting the ball over 110mph. That's fast. A lot of people may tell you that "baseball ready" is having your hands on your knees, looking ready for the ball. I hate that. "Baseball ready" is not resting with your hands on your knees. If you watch the big leaguers, you will see every player in the infield take one step in towards the batter and bend their knees in an athletic position. Their glove and throwing hand will be out in front of them, not on their knees. It's awesome to watch all of them get into that position at the same time. They all move their feet as the pitch is being thrown. NOT after the pitch. The outfielders may not bend and set up as low as infielders, but they do get into a position ready to move at that same time.

The bottom line is you need to be in a position as if you know the ball is being hit to you even if it's not. Don't wait until the ball is hit to see where it is going. That's too late. You will never get a good jump on the ball. You must want and think that the ball is coming to you and be ready for it.

Let's talk about backing up throws. As I said before, every player on the field should be or at least look like they are involved in every play. Backing up throws is such a big part of playing the outfield and one of the hardest things to teach young players. Many players, especially if you are in the outfield, feel that they don't have to move if the ball is not hit to them.

Baseball is a game of lines and angles. You must see the line the ball is traveling on after it is hit. You must move to that line or create an angle to cut the ball off by getting ahead of it. If a ball is hit to the outfielder next to you, you must also run to the ball and back up the play. What if the other player misjudges the ball? If they have the backup, there is someone there to pick up the ball and get it in. That backup play may save the game. If a ball is hit in the infield and an infielder has a routine play, the outfielder on that side still runs in toward the ball to provide backup in case of a missed play.

Remember, anything can affect the play, a bad hop, the infielder doesn't keep their glove down, or just a hard-hit ball that gets past the infield. So, an example of backing up throws-a batter hits a hard ground ball right at the shortstop, the ball takes a bad hop and gets past them. The runner sees that and makes a hard turn rounding first base. Following the rule of thumb, the outfielder backing up the shortstop fields the ball and comes up throwing to second. Let's see what everyone else should be doing. Following the lines of throws, the ball being thrown from left field to second base will follow a line that the right fielder and first baseman have positioned themselves for a possible backup. Let's pretend the worst. The left fielder throws to second base, but the second baseman misses the throw; the runner is safe at second but runs toward third because of the bad throw. The left fielder may think their job is over, but no.

Now, they must run to back up a possible throw from the right fielder to third base. The last thing a coach wants to see is a ball being thrown around without making any outs. It's a lot to follow, but a players' big mistake is assuming that plays will be made. I always taught my players, especially at the younger ages, to assume the play won't be made, and you need to be in a position to back it up. Even the best players can make an error. Another time for outfielders to be ready to back up throws is on steals. Right fielders back up throw to first if a runner is taking too far of a lead.

Center fielder backs up throws to second base from the catcher on a steal attempt or a throw from the pitcher on a pickoff attempt. Left fielders back up throws to third on steal attempts. It is tough for the outfielders to back up pick-off attempts on first and third because of the angle and how fast it happens, but they still need to be aware and ready to move if a ball gets by. Always know where the ball is from the time it leaves the pitcher's hand until they are ready to throw the next pitch and everywhere in between. By knowing who has the ball and through baseball awareness see where the play may be going. Get in the line that the ball will be going and be ready to back up a throw if necessary. Wow, look how much we have talked about the outfield! I hope you can see now how important playing the outfield is. There is a lot of room out there, and that is where games can be lost or won.

Routine singles that turn into triples, plays not being backed up, and runners score when they shouldn't. I will say it again and probably many more times throughout this book-baseball is a situational game, and the more you practice different situations the more baseball awareness you will have. I am only giving you rules of thumb to give you a foundation to start from. To give you an idea of what to do with a ball hit to you, one of the best things I did as coach was practice game situations that happened in our last game. So, whether we won or lost a game, at the next practice we would discuss the good and the bad situations that came up in that game and practice what we did right and what we did wrong. One of the drills we would do is to practice routine plays but have a position player who is set to receive a throw purposely miss the throw and watch the line the ball traveled on after the missed throw. By following that line, they could clearly see who should have been in position to back up the throw. For example, no one on base, and the batter lays down a beautiful bunt down the first base line. It's close enough for the catcher to field the ball. The catcher picks up the ball and fires it to first base. The person covering first purposely misses the throw. Where did the missed all go?

Of course, it ended up down the right-field line. Now, if the right fielder reacted to the bunt by running in and anticipating the throw to first, they would be in a position to back up that missed throw and keep the runner from advancing. If they think they have no play on a bunt and stay still on the play, well, now that ball ends up way down the line and the right fielder must chase it down and make a long throw to get it back in. By that time, the runner may be on third base, a triple from a bunt. Think about that. All because the outfielder thought the play was too far away from them and did not react. Same situation if the catcher tries to throw someone out at third. Even on a bunt, you must react as if the ball is coming to you. Be ready to move. So, is the outfield important? You better believe it.

CHAPTER 4

FIRST BASE

I am not going to say that one position is more important than another. What I will say is some positions have different skill sets than others. Just like having the skill sets of speed and a strong arm may make you a good outfielder, height, and flexibility may help make you a good first baseman. A first baseman will see throws coming from all directions, and they need to be able to get into the correct position quickly to make or complete a play. The height helps with covering as much of the area at first base as possible. When there is a close or hurried play at first, a fielder may rush a throw, and that throw may not be as accurate as they would like it to be. The first baseman must be able to track that throw and get in the best position to receive the throw to get the out.

They may have to stretch to get their glove out as far as possible so that the ball reaches their glove before the runner reaches the base. This takes training to be able to do. They may have to reach high in the air on a high throw. They may have to play a ball that bounces before it reaches their glove. When that happens, it is called a short hop, and the first baseman must scoop the ball up after the bounce. You may hear a coach yell "pick it" during the throw because they know the ball will not reach, and the first baseman will have to play the bounce or short hop. A first baseman will also have to know when to leave contact with the base and play the ball. Too often, we see younger players keep their foot in contact with the base when a bad throw is out of their reach. It is better that the runner is safe at first because you played the ball rather than playing the base and letting the ball get past you on a bad throw. If the ball does get past you, hopefully, the right fielder and catcher are playing heads-up baseball and are heading into a backup position where they can cut the ball off and prevent a disaster.

By disaster, I mean that dreaded triple that occurs because a missed play turns into extra bases. Once again practice increases baseball awareness as well as position awareness. If you practice enough and spend a lot of time playing a position, you start to develop the instinct for that position. You will just know where the base is as you quickly adjust to make a play. Your footwork will adjust to be in the best position. You will know when you must stretch to make that close play work in your favor.

First base is one of the two corner positions where you must be on your toes and ready to make a play. The ball will get on you fast because you are so close to the batter, and you need to stay relatively close to the bag to make a play. Your range isn't as big as shortstop or second base. The middle infielders have much more ground to cover and can change their distance from the batter as the situation dictates. Like I said before and will say several more times, you must be ready for the ball.

When the pitcher is set and starts his delivery to the plate, you must get in that baseball-ready position. Again, watch the pros. They all take that step in, bend their knees, gloves out in front, not resting on their knees. You will also notice their throwing hand is out in front as well. Their weight is on the ball of their feet, not leaning back on their heels. This is so they can spring into action after the batter makes contact. Notice I say AFTER the batter makes contact, not after the ball is in play. If you are not ready to react on contact, you will be too late when the ball is already in play. This will again come with practice and experience. It's called getting a good jump on the ball.

There are many factors that can help a fielder get a good jump on a ball after contact and even before contact. Again, we hear the term "baseball awareness". If you are paying close attention to the game and the players, there are several things you may notice. For instance, how is your pitcher pitching? Is their fast ball too fast for this batter? Is their curveball working today? Is their changeup working? Where is the batter set up? Are they off the plate? Close to the plate? Are they in front of the batter's box? Are they in the back of the box? Where in the batting order are they batting? Are they the leadoff batter? When they may be looking to walk or bunt for a hit?

Lead-off batters are trying to get on base in any way they can and are usually very fast runners. The number 3, 4, or 5 hitters, usually try to hit for power. Does the batter tend to swing early or late? These are all the things that every player should be paying attention to throughout the game. After the first time around the batting order, you will know how most of the players approach the pitches. I say most because maybe someone walked and didn't get anything to swing at. So, all this information gives you, as the fielder, a little edge because you can have an idea where the ball might go based on this information.

For example, a ball hit late will most likely go to the opposite side of the field. A ball hit early will most likely be pulled. So, if a right-handed batter pulls a ball, that means they are swinging early and the ball will travel somewhere on the left side of the field. That could be to the shortstop, third base, or left field. If a batter swings late, the ball will likely go to the opposite field toward the right field.

So, first base, second base, and right fielders all must be ready to move. Of course, the center fielder is moving on all these hits because they are the back up for both left and right fielders. Once again, baseball being a situational sport, a first baseman may not have a lot of ground to cover but where they do set up can be crucial to the play. One example would be if there are no outs, no one on base, and you have the leadoff batter up at bat, you may want to play closer to the batter in case a hitter squares for a bunt attempt. Some first basemen play as far up as the infield grass or closer.

As a corner position player, you will need to charge the ball on a bunt attempt. If the ball is bunted down the first base line, you must charge the ball to make the play, and hopefully, your pitcher or second baseman is covering the bag. If the ball is bunted down the third base line, you will be out of position to receive the throw at first, so again; hopefully, your pitcher or second baseman is there to cover the bag. You may expect a bunt with runners on the bases as well. As a matter of fact, you will see more bunt attempts with runners on the bases. The idea is that playing a bunt requires more time to make a play, so it is easier for a runner on base to advance to the next base on a bunt. The advantage the runner on base has is that they are already in motion by getting a lead before the pitch is thrown and getting a secondary lead after the pitch is thrown.

At the younger levels, there may not be any leading before the pitch but even that lead you get after the pitch reaches the batter is enough to get you to the next base faster than the ball can be played on a bunt. In most cases, a fielder will get the sure out at first, allowing the runner to advance. Trying to prevent the runner on base from advancing, typically requires a rush throw, which increases the odds of making a bad throw. Instead of getting the sure out at first, you may throw the ball away, and not only will all runners be safe you may have allowed a run to score. Another example of where a first baseman may set up is if you have a runner on first with one out.

Where you play in this situation may depend on who is at bat, the inning, and the score, but most of the time, you will be holding the runner on at first. If a ball is hit to you, you can possibly make a double play. The question is, do you throw to second base first, or do you step on first base and then throw to second? The answer is you let the ball decide depending on where the ball goes and where it takes your momentum. If it takes you back toward first and you can simply just step on the bag. It's a quick play and you still may have time to make the throw to second for the second out.

The problem there is that by getting the first out at first base, the runner advancing to second is no longer forced and must be tagged out. It's a much tougher play. It is always a tougher play to make when you must field a ball in the opposite direction from where you need to throw it. Here is another scenario, what if the ball is hit right at you or to the second base side of you? Well, now you attempt the forced double play. You field the ball and throw to second, and then your shortstop will fire the ball back to first base to complete the double play. Hopefully the pitcher will be there to cover the bag for that double play if need be.

Sometimes the second baseman can cover the bag depending on where they were at the start of the play. Another example of where a first baseman may set up is back behind the bag. This gives you the ability to cover more ground because you have more time to react by being a little further away from the batter. You may want to play back when there is very little chance of a bunt attempt, such as when there are two outs, two strikes, or a power hitter is up. Holding a runner on at first base is another very important job for a first baseman.

If you don't hold a runner on, they can take much bigger leads, which makes stealing second base much easier. So, holding a runner on keeps the runner from taking too far of a lead, but it also puts the first baseman in a position where they really need to be paying attention. The pitcher can decide to make a pickoff attempt at any time with no warning. That ball will be thrown fast, and you may have to adjust to catch it. You also must catch it in a position where you can tag the runner out if they are leading too far. You must be able to recognize the difference when the pitcher is going home with the pitch or a pickoff attempt.

This comes with knowing your pitcher and practicing it together. There is one rule that is a tremendous help to both the first baseman as well as the runner. A right-handed pitcher cannot have contact with the pitching rubber when they make the throw to first base on a pickoff attempt. With this rule for righties, their right foot must first disengage from the mound before they can throw. Now, as a runner, don't let that rule fool you into thinking you have more time to get back to the bag.

Some pitchers make that move very quickly, and the next thing you know, you're out. The rules are different for a lefty pitcher. A lefty pitcher can keep in contact with the rubber but cannot step toward home. This pickoff move is made by either just throwing the ball over to first with no other movement or by lifting the stride leg up and stepping toward first base rather than stepping toward home. When the lefty pitcher is facing the runner on first, they are in a better throwing position to get the ball over to first more quickly than righty pitchers. Therefore, a runner may not take as big a lead with a lefty pitcher on the mound. We will now circle back to the first baseman's job on a pickoff. We said that you must be in a position to catch the ball thrown by the pitcher, but where is that position?

Most of the time it's in front of the bag on the inside corner. Since a pickoff attempt is not a force play, the runner must be tagged out attempting to return to the base. A good base runner will take a far enough lead off first base, so they have to dive back head and hands first to make it back before the tag. You must be able to catch the ball and put the tag on before they get back.

Remember it is not that simple to do. There are several steps. The pitcher must have a good pickoff move; then, the throw must be accurate. You must give your pitcher a good target by holding your glove out in front of you. Since the runner is diving back, the tag will have to be made very close to the ground. A high throw from the pitcher won't make it. It must be a low throw towards the spot where the tag will have to be made. That spot is the inside of the bag. It is a race between your glove and the runner's hand or foot.

Some players make the mistake of trying to tag the runner and, most of the time, miss.

It is important to remember it will be tough for a runner to touch the bag if your glove is there first. Simply swipe your glove down to the spot on the bag that the runner must touch, and they will do the work for you by sliding or diving right into your glove. An experienced or well coached runner will slide to the back corner of the base because it forces the first baseman to have to reach further to make the tag. You will see many left-handed players playing first base because they have an easier reach to tag runners out on pickoff attempts. They also have an easier throw to second with less body movement.

Sometimes, you will see a first baseman play back behind the runner. This position may look like the runner is not being held on, but when pitchers, catchers, and the first baseman practice together and are on the same page, a timed pickoff attempt can be made. This happens when the runner thinks they are not being held on. The first baseman sneaks behind the runner and receives a well-timed throw from either the pitcher or catcher-which reminds me a catcher can also attempt a pickoff at any base after they catch a pitch. If the catcher sees that a runner's secondary lead is too far, the catcher can throw down to a base and try to pick the runner off. Sometimes, if the runner is caught off guard and can't get back to the base in time, they will be caught in a run down.

Most first basemen will use a first baseman's glove. The glove is larger than an infielder's glove to give a bigger target for the ball being thrown to first. It also has a unique curved edge, which greatly helps the first baseman scoop balls thrown in the dirt. The design also helps funnel the ball into the pocket and helps keep the ball from getting away. So why wouldn't all the infielders use this type of glove? Well, the other infielders need to make plays and transfer the ball from their glove to their throwing hand as quickly as possible. Having a bigger glove will slow down that transfer. The last thing I will say about first base is that many players think that once a runner passes first base, you are out of the play. That is not true; if a runner is going to second and there is a play from left field, follow the line of the throw. The throw may be off, and you should be in a position to back that throw up along with the right fielder. Now, you also may think that the cutoff men are only your middle infielders- not true. The first baseman should be in a cutoff position for throws going home from the right fielder as well as from center field. The rest of the infielders will be covering their bases.

CHAPTER 5

SECOND BASE

We have talked about different skill sets for different positions. Second base requires good baseball IQ or awareness. Not only do you need to know where the ball goes on any given play, but you also have a big cutoff position. You must know when you are required to cover second base, cover first base, or be the cutoff for a ball thrown from the outfield. There is a lot of ground to cover in this middle infield position, you must cover from second base all the way back close to first base.

Like we said earlier, a first base player can't travel that far away from first because they have to cover the base on most plays to first. To be a good second-base player, you must be fast and have quick reflexes. We also talked about getting a good jump on a hit ball. Just like the outfielders who have the most ground to cover, the better you are at getting a good jump on a ball, the more likely you will be in position to make a play. Second basemen do have the advantage of being able to adjust where they position themselves because of the range they are responsible for.

Once again, using baseball awareness and paying close attention to the game you may have an idea what pitches the batter will attempt to hit and where they tend to hit. Are they a pull hitter or more opposite field? If the batter is more of a pull hitter, you can play over towards second base. If they are an opposite-field hitter, you can play closer to first base. Which way the batter hits the ball can also depend a lot on your pitcher's speed and ball movement. So again, you need to know your pitchers. You also need to be aware of the batting order.

A leadoff batter may bunt; if so, the first baseman should be charging in to make the play on the ball. Someone then must cover first base; depending on where you were playing that batter, you may have to cover first base. I can mention different situations all day long, but this book would be endless if I did. We will stick to basic and the more common situations. Good coaching will let younger players know where to play based on many factors, such as the inning, the score, runners on base, the outs, the pitch count, and the batter. So, with all those factors, you can probably imagine how many different situations there could be. When would you not expect a batter to bunt?

Most coaches will instruct batters not to bunt with two strikes or two outs, or they may not bunt when there is a huge gap in the score. For example, if your team is winning 10-0, I would not have anyone bunting. Ok, so back to second-base responsibilities. You have to cover second base on force plays to second, but not all the time. Covering second base is shared with the other middle infielder, the shortstop. The rule of thumb is that for any ball hit to the shortstop side of the field or left field side, the second baseman must cover second base. If the ball is hit to the right field side, you must either make the play or, if the ball gets past you, you have to run to a spot to be the cutoff player.

Some younger players may run to just any spot, waiting for a throw. There is much to practice with the art of a relay play. A relay play is where there is a long throw needed to a particular base and there is a cutoff man required to complete the play. Yes, some players have the arm to reach far distances, such as outfielders, but not all throws will be in a direct line to a base especially from a hard thrower. When a ball is thrown hard, it may have some movement to it, meaning it starts off traveling online with the target but because of the fast rotation of the ball, the ball curves slightly off target. That's where a cutoff man can catch that ball and put it back online with the target. The cutoff also helps get the ball to the target more quickly if it does not have the distance to reach. It's ok for a ball to bounce once or twice before reaching the target, if it is on target. If it bounces too many times, then the ground will slow the ball down too much to beat out a runner.

Communication is the key. The example I will use here is a ball hit to right field with a runner on first and no outs. It's a close game, and you do not want that runner to score. So, using the rule of thumb that any ball hit to an outfielder, your first thought should be two bases ahead of the lead runner. With that in mind, a runner on first base will easily make it to second most of the time on a ball hit into right and will be looking to go to third base if the third base coach gives them the sign to keep running. So, the play is at third. The second baseman sets up about halfway between where the right fielder fields the ball and third base.

On some occasions, the ball may get hit so far that you may need a double cut. Communication starts right after the ball is hit, and everyone knows where it is heading. The third baseman knows the play is coming to them. Hopefully, the coaches are helping the younger players by letting them know where the play is going. The second baseman then starts to listen for the third baseman on where to line up for the cutoff. Remember we said baseball is a game of lines and angles? The ball will get to its target much faster by traveling in a straight line rather than creating angles. The third baseman will be yelling to the second baseman to move left or right to create that straight line.

Now, the second baseman is in position and should have their hands up high in the air so the right fielder easily sees them and knows where to throw the ball. The cutoff person should always try and catch the throw on their glove side and turn to that side so the transition is easier to throw, and they can keep their momentum as they turn to make the throw. If you turn to the opposite side of your glove, you must stop to shift your momentum. Your throw will take longer and will not be as strong.

Now, of course, you may see the pros make that throw without the use of a cutoff, especially on close plays but remember that is after many years of training and practice. I said that a ball will get to a target faster, traveling in a straight line. That is also true for the ark of the throw. Some younger players, especially younger catchers, want to reach the target, and taking into account the arm strength of those young players, the ball will have to have a huge ark to reach the target. It is very hard to teach young players that even if a ball bounces, it will get to the target faster on a straight line with as little ark as possible. The tough part about that is the receiving player must be able to play that bounce. It is a drill that some teams practice, but many don't.

Players who really want to improve their skills can practice those types of drills on their own. Just get a coach or friend to throw baseballs on a straight line to you at a base but intentionally bounce it to you. Every position player should practice scooping short hops as much as possible. This drill will help you judge ground balls better. It helps catchers as well as first basemen who see a lot of short hops. So far, regarding playing second base we talked about the range. We talked about covering two bases. We talked about being a cutoff man.

Let's talk about covering second base on steals. There are times younger players forget, or they are not sure who should be covering the base on a steal. Often, coaches will see the shortstop and second baseman look at each other, waiting to see who is covering. Unfortunately, that can result in no one covering the base. That drives catchers crazy. Some catchers will automatically throw the ball down. Well, your center fielder better be paying attention or that steal will be a run scored. Again, we have another rule of thumb: with a right-handed batter up, the second baseman should cover the base on a steal; with a left-handed batter up, the shortstop should cover.

The reason is that, statistically, batters tend to pull more balls than hit to the opposite field. Yes, this isn't 100%, and we have this rule of thumb solely based on stats and percentages. So, based on those stats, if a second baseman is running to cover second on a steal with a lefty batter up, he will be caught out of position on a pulled-hit ball. You want to play the percentages and keep the player in position based on the batter. Situations may change this rule of thumb, as with all baseball rules of thumb. When you are the player covering on a steal, be sure to play the ball and not the base. If it's a bad throw you don't want the runner advancing to third. The catcher should not be throwing the ball at you; that is to say that you are not the target.

A good catcher throws the ball to the right side of the base on a hard, low-line throw. This is where the runner will be sliding. It is the fielder's job to be there to receive the throw and make the tag. Many younger players throw to the fielder and end up throwing the ball behind the fielder, and the ball goes into the outfield. Remember, the fielder is on the run as well as the base runner so it is difficult to get that timing perfect. If everything goes perfectly, the catcher makes a good throw to the right side of the bag, and the fielder is there to receive it. The fielder can then put their glove in between the runner and the base. If the glove is in front of the base, the runner will slide right into it instead of touching the base first.

The worst thing you can do is try to tag the player higher up on his body or chase him. That's when players end up safe because they slide under or around the tag. If there is a runner on second you may also have to hold them on. This is a little different from holding a runner on at first base where the first baseman stays close to first with his foot touching the bag. Holding a runner on at second is more of an "in and out" technique. The second baseman or shortstop will jump back and forth toward the base, letting the runner see they are close enough to make a play if the pitcher decides to attempt a pickoff. The speed at which a second baseman or shortstop can get back into position when he is sure the pitcher is throwing to the plate is important. You must be quick to be ready for a throw from the pitcher or a ball hit after the pitch is thrown. The catcher may also throw down to second if they see the runner goes too far off the base. You must also be ready for that.

CHAPTER 6

SHORTSTOP

Working our way around the field, we get to the shortstop next. Shortstop is the other middle infield position where you need to cover a lot of ground. A shortstop needs to be able to cover that ground as well as a second baseman but also needs to have a strong arm. Throws from the shortstop position are further away from first base and require a stronger throw. With longer throws comes the risk of less accurate throws. So, a shortstop needs to be able to make the play from many different spots while making an accurate throw. It's a position where most coaches will put someone who is very athletic.

Shortstops need to be athletic because there is less time to make a throw to first being so far away. They need to be able to get a good jump on a ball at contact so they can field the ball quickly which will help to give them time to make a better throw. They have a lot of ground to cover so the throws can be from many different distances. Since there are more right-handed batters, especially at the younger ages, shortstop is a very busy position. They must field the balls hit to them as well as be the cutoff for throws coming in from the left fielder and center fielder. They will be listening for directions from the fielder at the base where the play needs to be made. Remember, the throw needs to be set up to be in a straight line. There are responsibilities of a shortstop that are the same as a second baseman regarding cutoff positions and responsibilities, but they are mostly the same only on the left field side of the diamond. I would rather move right into double plays.

Another very important part of being a middle infielder is turning double plays. Double plays are so much fun and exciting to watch. They happen very quickly, and everyone involved needs to be on their game to make it work. A routine double play happens when there are runners on base who are forced to run to the next base on a hit ground ball. Remember I said routine double play here are so many other situations where a double play can happen, but we will cover some others later. We are talking now about a ground ball hit in the infield with runners on base who are forced to run to the next base. For example, we will use the most common double play, where there is a runner on first with less than two outs.

This is a situation where baseball awareness will help players at each position be in the best position to make a play. The third baseman will be playing up, but since there is a runner on first the first baseman will be holding that runner on and not be playing up. If a bunt attempt results in a slow roller down the first baseline, the pitcher may have a better chance at fielding it. Second and shortstop can play back and pinch toward the middle to make the double play a little easier. As we have seen in different scenarios, knowing the situation and batter will help guide you with positioning. A ball gets hit on the ground to the shortstop.

They field the ball and quickly throw the ball, the second baseman covering second for the first out. The second baseman then must quickly throw the ball to first base to get the second out and successfully complete the double play. Sounds easy, right? It's not. I like to use 4 seconds as a good timing measurement for how long it takes a batter to run to first after a hit ball. Yes, some may be faster or slower, but 4 seconds is a fair time. So, to make a double play work it must be completed from the time the ball is hit to the time the runner reaches first base in under 4 seconds. With that in mind, there are many factors that could cause the double play not to be made.

Some examples are: a slow hit ground ball, a ball hit a little away from the first play where it takes an extra second to field the ball, bad ball transfer for either fielder trying to throw the ball, or maybe the batter running to first is fast. You will see more double plays being made the older you get because of baseball awareness, experience, athleticism, and arm strength. That's why the pros are so good at it. They are positioned well and have practiced it thousands of times in their career. I can use this play to demonstrate how the other fielders who think they are out of the play are, in fact, in the play and need to be in a position to back up any throwing or fielding errors.

Looking back at the situation, runner on first, one out. A batter hits a ground ball to the shortstop. The left fielder needs to be on the run to back up that play. The center fielder is on the run to back up the left fielder or vice versa, depending on where the ball is hit. The right fielder knows that there is a chance for a double play and that the shortstop will be throwing the ball to the second baseman to get the first out. The right fielder needs to be on the run to back up that throw. Again, remember to look for the line the ball will be traveling on with that throw. The catcher knows that to complete the double play the second baseman needs to fire that ball to the first baseman. So the catcher is also on the run to back up that throw. The third baseman moves to cover their base in case one of the throws gets away. They need to be ready for a possible play at third. The pitcher will be ready to back up either third or home, depending on how the play unfolds. So, a simple routine double play just involved all 9 players.

That is a routine double play, which they call a "6-4-3" because of the positions involved in making the play. There are many situations where a double play can be made. Bases loaded, and the first play goes home then to first base, a line drive right at a player, and they can catch the runner going back to a base. These are just a few of many. One thing I will tell you to practice a lot without getting into the mechanics of turning double plays or plays in general, is ball transfer. What I mean by ball transfer is how fast you can get the ball from your glove to your throwing hand, keeping control the entire time. Some really good players will not actually even catch the ball being thrown but instead use the glove to slow the ball down and redirect it into their throwing hand. There are drills for that. As you can see there are a lot of responsibilities for middle infielders. They also need to be able to communicate with each other as well as the pitcher and catcher. It helps the pitcher to know who is receiving the ball on a ball hit back to them with a runner on first. It helps the catcher to know who is covering the base on throws down to second on steal attempts. This is more for the younger players because as you get older and have more experience, the catcher is hitting a spot on the base, and someone needs to be there. Communication is key. Before the next pitch, make sure everyone is on the same page.

CHAPTER 7

THIRD BASE

Third base is the other corner position. It's a position that requires fast reflexes and a strong arm. Except for the pitcher, the corner positions are the closest to the batter. You can argue that the catcher is the closest, but the batter isn't trying to hit the ball in the direction of the catcher. That position we will cover next. As for third base, it is also considered the "hot corner." This is because, like I said earlier, most hitters are right-handed batters and pull the ball. When a ball is hit hard towards third base, it gets there fast. A player needs to be on their toes and ready to receive it. Having quick reflexes helps the player react to the ball and make quick moves in the direction the ball travels. That could be left, right, in, out, or even a diving play to keep the ball in the infield.

You need a very good arm for third base as it is a far throw to reach first before the runner. Remember, you must field the ball, transfer it to your throwing hand and reach first all in under 4 seconds. For the most part, third base is more concerned with playing in or back more than left or right. Having a good shortstop helps the third baseman not have to worry about balls hit in the gap between them. The third baseman will sometimes look like they are stealing a play on a ball hit toward the shortstop. This happens a lot on slow-hit balls, which allow time for the third baseman to get a jump on the ball.

Plays are made more easily when your momentum is going toward your target. So, a third baseman fielding a ball while their momentum is going towards first base is an easier play than the shortstop running in for it or having to change direction to make the throw. This is a good time to point out practice, communication, and getting to know your teammates. With the experience of playing together, you will know what to expect each other to do in different situations. At third base, you need to be aware of runners on second for a possible steal attempt, which is not that common but happens, especially if players are not paying attention.

You need to be aware of runners on third for a possible pickoff coming from either the pitcher or catcher. You need to pay attention to who's up in the batting order for a possible bunt situation. Should you be playing up, should you be back, or maybe even with the bag? One of the most impressive plays and hardest plays to execute is the "5,4,3" double play. That's a ball hit to third, throw to second, and then to first. Everything must be right. The ball must be hit hard enough; the third baseman needs to field it cleanly, have a quick transfer, and get the ball over to second as fast and as accurately as possible; then, the second baseman needs to do the same and get the ball over to first.

Again, all in under 4 seconds. One important skill a third baseman must have is knowing when NOT to throw the ball. Sometimes, you see a weak ground ball that the third baseman must hustle in for and make a dramatic throw to first base. It looks awesome when it works but spells disaster when it doesn't. That kind of hurried throw on the run requires many years of practice to get it right. Otherwise, the ball ends up way down the right field line, and that runner will quickly be rounding second and probably on his way to third. You must hope that you have a heads-up right fielder who understands the risk of that throw and is already running in for the backup before the ball is thrown. With practice, many third basemen can make that play barehanded to be able to get a quicker throw to first. It is not recommended for younger ages. We want them to get used to using gloves first.

Chapter 8

Catcher

Now that we have talked about the 7 positions in the field that require a tremendous amount of thought, practice, and experience, we move to probably the toughest physical position on the field. The catcher. The responsibilities of the catcher seem endless. First, they are the only players on the field who can see the entire field and all the possible runners on base from their position. At younger ages, the coach, the other players, as well as the parents and fans in the seats, will be yelling where to throw a ball that is hit. That is bad for a catcher especially because sometimes they are not all yelling to throw the ball to the same place.

As you get older, that responsibility is left more to the catcher, or at least it should be. Again, they can see the whole field, the angle a ball was hit, and where the runners are. When a ball is hit, you will hear a catcher yell out the number of the base, they feel the ball should be thrown to. For example, if a ball hit on the ground in the infield with no one on base, they will be yelling, "One, one, one." If it gets past the infielders, they know the rule of thumb of two bases, so they will be yelling, "Two, two, two." If it is a good hit that goes in the gap past the outfielders, they will yell, "Three, three, three." This is another example of situational baseball.

There are many reasons why a catcher will yell out bases for plays to be made. It could be the speed of the runners, the score, the inning, or a number of other reasons. Having that rule of thumb is a great place to start. As important as it is for every player on the field to know their pitchers, it is especially important for the catcher. At younger ages, the coaches will more than likely be calling the pitches they feel the pitcher needs to throw for a particular hitter in different situations. What I mean by calling pitches is someone deciding what the next pitch should be. For example, fastball, curveball, changeup, or any other pitch. The catchers will then give the pitchers signs using their fingers held between their knees, low and out of view, so only the pitcher can see them.

Some catchers will even paint their fingernails or use colored tape to enable the pitcher to see the signs more easily. Usually in high school, the responsibility of calling pitches becomes the catcher's job. There are two main reasons why the catcher gives signs to the pitcher on what pitch to throw. One is so the catcher knows what to expect as the ball is being thrown. The other is because they might know what pitches a particular batter has trouble with. They need to be able to move to a position where they can expect the ball to travel. This is so they can catch the ball cleanly and, more importantly, keep the ball in front of them and not let it get behind them, which could allow runners on base to easily advance to the next base or even score.

Fastballs move enough, but trying to catch a good curveball or slider can be challenging, especially if the ball's movement causes the ball to bounce before the catcher gets their glove on it. Now remember, this is all done with full catcher's gear on, including a face mask which partially blocks your vision. The pitch the catcher calls is based on many factors, most of all the batter at the plate and game situation. The first time through the batting order is the learning phase for the catcher.

Is the batter being aggressive and swinging the bat? Are they leaving the bat on their shoulders, waiting to walk? Are they fast runners who may be looking to bunt? Is a power hitter swinging for the fences? Are they late on the fastball? Are they early?

All the things a catcher needs to pay attention to, so the next time batters get up, the catcher has a better idea of what pitches to throw. Typically, especially at younger ages, most pitchers can control their fastball better than other pitches they may throw. That's because other pitches should have more movement, and it takes time to control where that movement will take the ball. A fastball is meant to be a pitch you can throw for a strike that is tough for a batter to hit because of the speed. Hopefully, the first pitch is a strike, so you can be ahead in the count to start.

Most kids at younger ages will not swing at the first pitch they see, which, by the way, I hate when coaches teach kids to take pitches until they get a strike. We will talk about that later when I get into hitting, but why would you give the pitcher the opportunity to get ahead in the count? If you see the first pitch as a pitch you can hit, swing the bat. The first time through the batting order should be an advantage to the pitcher. I say this because the batter hasn't seen how hard you throw; they don't know how much your ball moves.

Do you have a good curveball or other off-speed pitch? Having the edge of the batter, not knowing your pitches, is a good time for a catcher to call different pitches. This way, they can see what pitches are working and if the pitcher has command of their pitches. This all helps for the next time around the order. If a pitcher has above average speed for the level of play they are at, well, that makes the pitch call easier for the catchers. There is a good chance that the hitters can't catch up to the speed so the call will be mostly fastballs. Even if the batters start to catch up after a few innings, it usually just requires a few off-speed pitches to throw their timing off again.

A good pitcher is someone who can throw a strike at any time when needed, but the better pitchers know the art of not throwing a strike. At the major league baseball level, if a pitcher throws a ball right down the middle, it usually results in the ball ending up 400 feet away in the seats for a home run. Catchers know this, so they are calling the pitches to hit different locations around the plate. Close enough to get the umpire to call it a strike but far enough away so that the batter can't get a good swing at it. Or at least not get the sweet spot of the bat on the ball. Another very important aspect of being a good catcher is your ability to block balls from getting past you. There are so many drills to help you be a better backstop. Yes, I said backstop. You never want that ball getting any further behind the plate than you.

Learning how to move to a ball, drop to your knees, and glove positions are very important. You must spend a lot of time practicing just this. It takes a long time for catchers to just stop turning their heads on balls in the dirt, trying to protect their faces. It's a natural instinct. But sometimes turning your head can be more dangerous because there is less protection on the side of the mask. I used to throw tennis balls at my catchers and have them put their hands behind their backs. They could only block the ball with their bodies. I would purposely throw at their face masks in order to teach the mind that they have the protection they need.

Let's talk about stealing a strike call. A good catcher knows how to steal strikes by doing what's called framing the pitches. It's a technique that should be taught as early as possible in a catcher's career behind the plate. The big mistake young catchers make is having their gloves follow the pitch. What I mean by this is as a pitch is thrown the catcher starts with their glove in the middle of the strike zone and then follows the ball movement as they're catching it out of the strike zone. This especially happens with off-speed pitches that tend to have the most movement.

What catchers need to do is the opposite. They should provide the pitcher with a good target, but as the ball is released, they should move the glove down and wait for the pitch. If the pitch is a little low, they should catch the ball with the glove moving up into the strike zone and hold it there. This means stopping the glove in the strike zone. Many times, an umpire will call the pitch a strike even though it was a little low.

This applies to any pitch a little out of the strike zone, whether it is a little high, a little low, a little inside, or a little outside. Obviously, your first job is to catch the ball, but have the glove moving toward the strike zone as you make the catch and not away. Speaking of umpires, the catchers are their best friends. They rely on the catcher to protect them from wild pitches and foul tips.

It is smart when the game starts to make sure you introduce yourself to the umpire and shake their hand. If an umpire does get hit by a missed ball or a foul ball, walk the ball out to the pitcher and give the umpire a minute to recover. They usually will do the same for you. I hear that someday; we may have electronic eyes calling balls and strikes. Until then, we have the umpire's judgment and must respect it. A good catcher will also see the balls that umpires call a strike and which ones are balls. This means different umpires may have different strike zones. As we get older, that strike zone gets smaller and smaller. Some umpires have a high strike zone, and some have a low strike zone. Some will give a pitcher the inside corner, and some will give the outside corner. It is up to the catcher to recognize which umpire they get and use that to the pitcher's advantage when selecting pitches and the location of pitches. It is so good for pitchers when they get that outside corner called for a strike.

Most hitters, especially younger kids, won't swing at an outside pitch. As you get older, it's more of the low pitches that get called strikes. I will cover more of this when we talk about pitchers. Let's talk about throwing runners out on steal attempts. A catcher needs to have quick reflexes, a very strong arm, and good instincts. One way they measure catchers is by using a term called "pop time." That is the time that a pitched ball hits the catcher's glove to the time it hits the player receiving the throw's glove.

A good pop time is 2.0 seconds. Under 2.0 seconds is above average. But having a good pop time does not make a catcher good. It helps tremendously, but a catcher must have all the skills I already mentioned, as well as baseball awareness. They need to know when to try and throw a runner out and when to just hold the ball. They may give the pitcher a sign to throw over to a base to keep runners close if they are taking big leads. They may throw down to a base themselves if they see a runner too far off a base.

A mistake that many young players make when trying to throw a runner out is throwing to the player receiving the ball and not the base. When trying to throw a runner out stealing second or third base the catcher's target is the right side of the base and as low as possible. If the ball is thrown accurately, all the receiver must do is catch the ball and put their glove between the runner and base. If the catcher tries to throw the ball to the receiver, who is usually still moving and getting in position, the throw will be off. If the catcher throws to the left side of the base, it makes the catch tougher for the receiver, and now they must reach to try and tag the runner. This usually doesn't work. A catcher throwing the ball to catch a runner stealing isn't concerned about where the receiver is on the attempt. They have a target, and it is the responsibility of the receiver to be there. This goes back to other players being baseball-aware.

Where should the outfielders be on a steal attempt? That's right-in a position to back up the throw. Whether the throw is to second or third, the outfielders need to see the runner going, make sure the hit and run isn't on, and then run in so they can back up a bad throw or a missed throw. Another mistake young catchers make is trying to reach second base on steal attempts. A ball will reach its target much faster on a low line than on an arc. Because younger catchers are trying to reach, they tend to throw the ball too high, which gives the runner more time to reach the base safely. I remember telling catchers repeatedly that it's okay if the ball bounces before the base as long as the ball is on target. I used to have them practice a controlled bounce if they couldn't reach a low line. This meant keeping your target on the right side of the base in mind and purposely throwing the ball about 6 or 7 feet before it.

If they throw too close, it becomes a short hop for the receiver and tough to catch. If they throw it too short and it bounces twice, it won't get there in time. By the way, that goes for throws from the outfield as well. Keep the ball low and on target. So, what makes a good catcher? Athleticism, arm strength, baseball awareness, ability to catch and block pitches, attention to hitter's strengths and weaknesses.

Communication on and off the field. The catcher should have the ability to keep pitchers calm and reassure them of their abilities. If a pitcher is not having their best day, a good catcher knows to call timeout and go talk to them. They can point out something they see a pitcher can do differently with their mechanics or something with the batter. Even if they say nothing at all, it gives the pitcher a chance to take a deep breath and maybe focus a little bit better.

CHAPTER 9

PITCHER

Pitches are the players who get the recorded wins or losses for the game. Even though this is a team sport, and we teach kids the philosophy of winning and losing as a team, the pitchers take the glory or the heat. As much as we can say that no one play causes a team to lose, we can also say that it wasn't the pitcher alone who caused the win. The team still needs to make plays and they need to score runs. Except for a perfect game pitched by a pitcher, every team can make mistakes and lose. I have seen teams lose games when a pitcher throws a no-hitter.

Runners get on base either by walks or fielding errors. They steal a few bases, and the next thing you know, they score runs. Here is an example- a pitcher has a no hitter going through six innings, and they walked the first two batters in the seventh. A passed ball lets the runners advance to second and third. The batter then hits a fly ball to center. The runner on third tags up. One run scores. If the ball is played correctly, the throw goes to third, keeping the runner on second right where they are. Ok, now there is one out with a runner on second who is fast and a good base stealer. They get a good secondary lead and steal third.

The batter hits another fly ball to the outfield, far enough for a tag up. Now the score is 2-0 with a no-hitter still going. Is this loss the fault of the pitcher? I don't think so. The team must support the pitcher by getting hits and scoring more runs than the other team. To lose a game 2-0 with a pitcher throwing a no hitter is rare but happens, and the team, not just the pitcher, lost that game. Even if a pitcher pitches a perfect game, the team still needs to score at least one run to win the game. Once again, it was a team win. Yes, the pitcher did an amazing job and got every hitter out with no walks, but the team still had to make plays and get runs to help secure the win.

Pitchers in general, must have a clear head on the mound and think about their job. Their job is to get batters out. That could be with a strikeout or a hit ball that gets played in the field for an out. I used to tell my kids at young ages I would rather be a pitcher that causes a hitter to hit ground balls and pop ups all day than to be a strikeout pitcher. If you can throw strikes and make batters swing the bats early, there is a good chance they will hit the ball where a play can be made. This can result in fewer pitches being thrown per inning, and you can use your arm to get through more innings, which in turn saves the coach from having to use other pitchers.

The coach can save those pitchers for the next game and have fresh arms. If you try to be a strikeout pitcher, you need to throw a minimum of 3 pitches per batter, which is 9 pitches per inning. That is great pitching, but it very rarely goes that way. You would typically throw more like 5 or 6 pitches per batter which would bring your pitch count up more quickly. That is not counting good at-bats for hitters where they get you to a full count and foul off the next 8 pitches. Now you just pitched 12 or 13 pitches to one batter. I encourage coaches and young players to learn two pitches: a good fastball that they can throw for a strike and a change-up just to keep the batters guessing. All the fancy curveballs, sliders, slurves, and cutters can be taught much later on when you actually **are** trying to strike batters out. I have seen kids throwing curveballs with every other pitch as young as 9 years old.

By the time they hit high school, their arms are shot. The kid who was the ace pitcher all through Little League now has to learn to be a better hitter and play first base because their elbow or shoulder hurts when they throw. The other mistake I see too often is when parents want to be their kid's only coach without having the knowledge or background to do so. Their kid has the gift of having a strong arm, so they will be a pitcher because they throw the ball harder than any of their teammates. Then their parent teaches them a curveball, and the kid is lights out throughout the little league. The things that were missing the whole time were teaching them the mechanics of pitching and arm care.

As a pitcher, you feel like everyone is relying on you. That you must be at your best at all times, that every pitch matters and that you have to get every batter out. Relax, it's not all up to you; you don't always have to be at your best, and you don't have to get every batter out. The idea is that you work hard off the field to be at your best for the games, but it doesn't always happen. It's part of being human, we are not always at our best. That goes for everything we do in life. You are not always going to be the best parent, the best kid, the best friend, the best worker, or maybe even the best boss someday. You certainly shouldn't be stressed about being the best player every time you're on the field, but it doesn't mean you don't try.

That's the idea that we try, that we learn, that we practice, that we work to be the best we can be at anything we love doing. It's not to impress other people but to impress ourselves that we can be better than we were yesterday. Go out there, get on the mound, and give it your best shot. Use what you have learned from your instructors and what you have practiced. If you're on, you're on, and if you're not, you didn't fail; you learned. You learned that even if you put out your best, it may be the hitter's day to shine.

Remember that they are working just as hard as you to be able to hit those pitches. One of the things a pitcher will have to be aware of is their pregame preparations. It is extremely important to have a proper warmup routine before you take the mound in any game. That is why it is important to have a good pitching coach who will teach you pre-game warmups and stretching routines. Please don't ever get on the mound cold, and parents, if you are reading this, please keep an eye out for this.

Too many times, I have seen coaches looking to win a game or trophy by putting kids in a game to pitch when they haven't stretched or warmed up. Some parents are ok with this because they may want the trophy more than their kids do, or they don't want to let their kids let the team down, or they just don't know any better.

It's game time. You're on the mound, and you're facing batters for the first time in their order. What pitches will the catcher call, you wonder. They might want to see how aggressive the batters are the first time around and call for fastballs. You both can see if the batters are swinging, hoping to walk or just seeing how fast you throw. But you want that first pitch to be a strike. You want them swinging, and you want to be ahead in the count. Now that the batter is behind in the count, you are hoping that they are looking to swing at the next pitch. Hopefully they miss or hit into a play that gets them out.

Remember, I said I would rather that happen at younger ages. It results in lower pitch counts. If this first pitch is a ball, most kids will take the next pitch to see if you **can** throw a strike. Getting the first strike is extremely important because you don't want to set the tone that you are struggling to throw strikes. The next batters up will be standing there waiting to walk and your pitch count gets high too quickly. If you can consistently get the first pitch strike, by the second time through the order, those batters will be swinging.

Now is the time to change things up. They know you can throw strikes; they have seen your speed and feel that they can time it out. If they do start to time your fastball, this is the time to show off that off-speed pitch you have been working on so hard. The slower speed throws off their timing, and if the ball has movement, their timing will be off even more.

Now, when you go back to your fastball, it will appear even faster to the batter. As the innings go on and you get more and more comfortable with your pitch location, you can really get them off balance. Hopefully, you have a good catcher who knows your stuff and can call the right pitches at the right moment. The good thing about the communication between a pitcher and a catcher is that you don't always have to throw what the catcher calls. If you think a better pitch will work in a particular situation, simply shake your head no to the catcher until he gives you the sign you are looking for. Of course, if the batter hits a home run on the pitch you called, well, it happens.

A good pitcher will show no emotions on the mound. Of course, with anything in life, you have your good days and your bad days. Even if you give up back-to-back home runs, you must stay cool and be ready to throw the first pitch to the next batter as if nothing happened. You still have a job to do. Until the coach decides to take you out you keep pitching your best. Showing emotion on the mound is admitting defeat, and you never want to show that to your teammates, your coaches, and especially the other team.

Remember, it's baseball, and anything can happen at any time. Maybe your team rallies and comes back to win the game. You can't expect your teammates to pick you up after a bad inning if you show them that you gave up. Walk off the mound the same way whether you struck out all three batters you faced, or you gave up 5 runs. It's tough to do, but it shows that you know it's baseball, and you can take the good with the bad.

Another job the pitcher has while on the mound is keeping runners close to the base making it harder for them to steal. Without runners on base or when you are not worried about a possible steal you will be most likely pitching from the full windup position. This is where some people think a pitcher generates more momentum therefore throwing harder. I can name some pro pitchers who never throw from the windup and throw 100 mph, but that's not the point.

A pitcher should throw from the position they are most comfortable in and have the most command of their pitches. You may be able to throw harder from the windup, but if you can't throw strikes, it doesn't help. The other position a pitcher will use is called the stretch position. This is where you stand sideways to the batter, and it requires less movement and less time to throw over to a base on pickoff attempts. Attempting to pick off a runner from the full windup position will result in a balk every time. A balk is when pitchers make a move that deceives the batter and runner by stepping towards the plate but throws the ball to a base instead.

A pitcher must come set or to a complete stop before throwing the pitch. Their hand and the ball must be in their glove for a full second when set. If they separate their hands too early or do not immediately throw the pitch, the umpire can call a balk. Basically, you can't fake throws to the plate or a base without throwing it from the mound. A right-handed pitcher must step off the rubber to make a pickoff attempt, but a lefty doesn't have to. A lefty does have to step toward the base they are throwing to. For example, if the lefty pitcher lifts their right leg to pitch and steps toward home, they must throw it home. If they step toward first, they can throw to first.

Balks are tricky, and all pitchers need to practice pickoff moves to prevent them. Balks can only occur with runners on base, and if they do occur, all runners on base move up one base. This could be bad if there is a runner on third who will now score. It's called having a good pickoff move. You can pick off a runner at any base, but first base is the most common. The reason is that you don't want a catcher to have to try and throw a runner out attempting to steal second base. It's the furthest throw a catcher must make when trying to throw a runner out. You don't want to allow the runner too much of a head start. If the pitcher or catcher, for that matter, thinks a runner is taking too far of a lead, the pitcher may throw over to first on their own, or the catcher may give them a sign to throw over. Not every throwover has to be a quick move and throw.

Sometimes you are just letting the runner know **you** are there and that you know **they** are there. Some pitchers, early in a game, will show a very slow pickoff move, leading the runner to believe they can take a bigger lead. The next time the pitcher uses their real pickoff move, you might just catch the runner sleeping. Developing a good pickoff move comes with practice, and hopefully, a good coach can give you some very helpful pointers. I will talk about pickoff moves again later when we discuss base running.

Again, I can't stress enough how important it is for a pitcher to stay cool and focused on the mound. Yes, you feel like the game is on your shoulders, but it's a team sport. When you do get into trouble in a game, take a second, take a deep breath, and remember a lesson where your coach addresses issues you may tend to have. Remember your mechanics; don't worry about speed. I never realized how much there is to learn about throwing mechanics.

The funny thing is I signed my son up for pitching lessons just to teach him how to properly throw a baseball. I had no idea he would turn into a pitcher. I just wanted someone with knowledge and experience to teach him the right way to throw so he could stay healthy and be more accurate. I wanted him to learn how to properly train, warm up, and take care of his arm. I went to every lesson, and I paid close attention to the coach so that I could help my son when he practiced on his own. I didn't realize at the time the number of small things that mean so much when throwing a baseball.

The grip, weight transfer, balance, posture, load, stride, arm path, hip rotation, hip/shoulder separation, front footstep, front leg blocking, release point, and follow through. It was great that he had a good little league coach (no, not me at first, lol) but a man who believed every kid deserves a chance to play at every position to see where they are more comfortable and may excel. When he started to use my son to pitch, I was surprised at how well he could throw strikes. He was not the hardest thrower on the team, but he could throw strikes. So, the coach started using him more and more, and he continued with the lessons and got better and better. By the time I started coaching his team, he was pretty good. Again, not the hardest thrower, but threw strikes. He would get a lot of batters out with ground balls and pop-ups.

When he turned 14, he was able to throw harder, and the travel coaches used him a lot to pitch in regular games but mostly in the championship games. He hit a growth spurt and went from 5'8" to 6'3" in one year. He started to really hit his stride in high school and played on the varsity team as a freshman. I just realized how long I have been writing this book. I mentioned that my kids were in sixth and eighth grade when I started writing. They are now in tenth and twelfth grade. Wow, time flies.

My older son, who just got a college scholarship to pitch at a D2 university, is very excited to play at a higher level. My younger son is also a pitcher and played on the varsity as a freshman too. They are both good hitters as well. He had just as many lessons as his older brother. It will be tough in college to hang the bats up, but they understand that all teams need more pitchers than position players. Watching both of my boys play from such young ages and taking an interest in how and what they are learning along the way made me understand what it takes to play this game. I became a student of the game.

From what I have learned through playing, coaching, umpiring, and research, I feel I really understand this game, especially from the mental aspect. I have learned to use this knowledge in my everyday life and in my career by teaching students that life is so much like this game. Every year, I tell them a baseball story about being a teammate or a co-worker and having family and friend's support.

CHAPTER 10

HITTING

Now, we move into the offense part of this game. Hitting. Again, not claiming to be a mechanics coach with any position on the field, but I was a pretty good hitter in my day. I have learned so much by watching the coaches work with my kids and through my own research. Hitting is the one time you are not relying on any of your teammates' help other than encouragement and support. It's you against the pitcher and eight other players in the field trying to get you out. I have always taught my kids that you may only get one good pitch to hit in any at-bat.

Early in the game, that may be the first pitch you see. Remember when we talked about pitchers wanting to get that first strike? You can be a hitter that likes to take first pitches to gauge how fast the pitcher throws but that might be the best pitch you see. I also tell the kids that you should be watching the pitcher warm up in between innings especially while you're in the on-deck circle. I realize it's a different look than when you are standing in the batter's box, but you should still be able to get a good read while waiting to hit.

Without getting into the mechanics of hitting you want to have a good presence at the plate. You want to show the pitcher that you are not afraid of any pitch that they may throw. Show you have confidence at the plate. Remember the last time you got a hit and bring that memory with you. I can't tell how many times I have heard kids say, "Wow, this pitcher is fast. I can't hit that."

Guess what, you **can't** hit that. Not with that approach – which brings up that word, approach. How you approach the plate when getting up to bat is very important. If you are thinking about the last three times this pitcher struck you out, you may just strike out again. Instead, think about the last game where you got a hit. It may have been five games ago but remember it and bring it with you. If you have faced this pitcher before, your odds of hitting off them go up because you have seen their pitches before. Remember, you may only get one good pitch to hit in an AB. What I mean by that is a pitch that you can handle.

It may be a ball up in the zone or down in the zone or something else that you know you hit better than other pitches. It may not even be a strike, but you like it. Swing the bat. If you see that pitch, swing the bat. I'll say it again, swing the bat. One of my biggest pet peeves is watching kids strike out looking. In my experience, kids tend to strike out looking at outside pitches more than anything else. Of course, umpires play a big role in what a strike is and how far outside they will call a strike, but if it's close enough to call a strike, it's usually close enough to hit. I have demonstrated how far a pitch can be off the plate and still be hit cleanly. I used to put a ball on a tee and have the kids practice hitting a ball in many different locations. High, low, inside, outside, and many more. I have put the ball on that tee as far as a foot off the plate and showed them it can still be hit cleanly.

Now, of course, I don't want or expect them to swing at a pitch a foot off the plate. It's just an example to teach them that they can hit a pitch thrown a little outside and not leave it up to the umpire to call strike three. Getting back to that word, approach. There are different approaches during an AB based on the pitch count, runners on base, and the pitches being thrown. As a batter, your job is to put the ball in play and get on base. Walking counts as getting on base. It helps your team to have runners on base.

Most of the time, walking is the result of pitchers not having command of their pitches. Sometimes, hitters will be intentionally walked if they are a big threat to drive in runs or if the defense wants to create runners to be forced out at any base. Usually this will only happen towards the end of a close game. For now, we will concentrate on the pitcher trying to get you out. It's you against the pitcher, and you have the confident approach that you are going to win the battle and get on base. As much as I emphasized swinging the bat earlier, there are times to be disciplined at the plate too. Maybe the game is close, and you need a runner on base. Maybe the pitcher is a little tired and not as sharp as they were earlier.

It's ok to take pitches, especially if you don't see the one you want. When you are ahead in the count you create more choices for your AB. You challenge the pitcher to throw you a strike. You can only do that for two strikes. A two-strike approach is different. Now, you not only have to worry about the pitcher, but you also must worry about the umpire. Maybe the umpire is pitcher-friendly and will call anything close a strike. You must be ready to swing and protect the plate with two strikes. You will hear teammates and coaches yell that out. "Protect the plate."

What that means is you don't have to wait for a pitch down the middle. You can swing at close pitches and try to put the ball in play; if you foul the ball off 10 times, it is better than striking out looking. Hitting is the biggest failure part of the game there is. When people make that statement about baseball being a sport of failure, this is what they mean. I mentioned earlier that you can get 1000 ABs and fail 700 times and be considered a great hitter. Learning how to accept that ratio is the tough part.

Hitting a baseball is exceptionally challenging, especially when you consider that it's a round object coming at you with high speed, and you're attempting to make contact with a round stick. As players advance in age, their batting averages tend to decrease because the pitches they face become faster, providing them with less reaction time to connect. Additionally, pitchers develop better ball movement over time. We can observe this trend clearly when we look at professional Major League players as an example.

We will use 90 mph as the speed of the pitch, even though some of today's pitchers are throwing 100. It is 60 feet 6 inches from the pitching rubber to home plate. The pitcher is releasing the ball even closer to the plate based on their mechanics. The hitter has about 150 milliseconds to decide to swing the bat. That is the speed of the blink of an eye. If they do swing, they still must hit the ball squarely with a round object. You may hear from time to time that a batter really timed that one, or they really squared that one up.

Reaction times are obviously much slower at younger ages, but it's all relative because the pitches are slower, as well as the bat speeds. Having a good hitting coach is essential when it comes to learning how to hit a baseball. A good coach will teach approach, stance, bat path, hand-eye coordination, load, weight shift, and follow-through. A coach will work on pitch recognition. You need to be able to follow a baseball from the pitcher's windup, through the release and see the contact of the bat and ball.

When the ball comes out of his hand, you may see the rotation of the baseball, which will help you decide where your bat path needs to be. This comes with years and years of seeing pitches. A fastball will have a backspin as it approaches you. A curveball will have a front spin. A knuckleball will have no spin. A pitcher's arm slot and release point will cause the ball to have different spin directions as well. All this causes the ball to move in different directions to try and fool the hitter into where the ball will be. You will eventually start to learn which pitches you like for your swing.

There are times in a game when you may come up to bat in a situation where you think you must get a hit. It could be a close game with runners in scoring position, or maybe the tying run is on third. I don't believe in trying to force a hit. That's when you are swinging at bad pitches to try and be the hero for your team. It could end up hurting the team.

Pitchers want you to swing at bad pitches because they know there is a better chance of you missing the ball or hitting it weakly to one of the players to get out. On the other hand, don't let good pitches go by in those situations because you may miss the chance to drive those runs in. Here is a situation where a player may swing at a bad pitch: a tie game in the later innings with a runner on third and less than two outs; all the hitters must do is hit the ball anywhere in the outfield, and the runner most likely scores. Getting a hit in that situation is great. Trying to force a hit on a bad pitch, resulting in an out, is not so good. I would rather see you walk. I know it's not glamorous or getting to be the hero, but now you have two runners on, and if the coach is smart, they have the runner on first steal second, so you now have two runners in scoring position. Remember, it's a team sport.

I want to touch on "sacrificing" at-bats. This is when an out results in a runner scoring or advancing bases. You can have a sacrifice fly where there is a runner on third, and you hit a ball far enough into the outfield that it gives the runner time to tag up at third and score. Even though you got out, it doesn't count as an official AB, so it doesn't hurt your batting average. Another way to sacrifice is to bunt. Bunting is an art. To be able to bunt a ball correctly takes a tremendous amount of practice. Again, if executed correctly and you advance the runner, it doesn't hurt your average when you get out.

One common mistake a batter makes when attempting to bunt is trying to push the ball or slightly swinging at the ball. The object is to try and catch the ball with your bat. The speed of the pitch will do all the work for you. Never reach down or up for the ball you're trying to bunt. You can square your body up and get into the bunt stance, but let your knees do the work of moving the bat up or down. If you must reach with the bat, then it's not a good pitch to bunt. You also can't have unlimited foul balls when bunting. If you have two strikes, you do not want to try bunting because if you foul it off, you're out.

You also do not have to keep the bat out during a bunt attempt. If you don't like the pitch, pull the bat back and take the pitch. There are a few different types of bunting. A standard bunt is where you square your body off to the pitcher, and everyone knows you're bunting; the drag bunt is where you hide the fact that you're bunting until the last second and then just stick the bat out as you start running. The squeeze play bunt is when the runner on third is coming down the line after a successful bunt. And finally, the suicide squeeze, where the runner on third starts running home before you contact the ball on a bunt attempt. This is the only time you will be trying to force a hit by chasing the ball.

You want to keep the catcher from catching the ball at all costs, or it's an easy out for the runner who has already committed to running home. Better to be a foul ball on a bad pitch than the out. Hitting is another time when you don't want to show emotion. You strike out, you strike out. No big deal. You get a hit; act like it's not your first time. You hit a home run don't show up the pitcher by celebrating too much. You hit the game-winning home run, well celebrate with your team, but do not direct anything negative to the other team. Enjoy the moment. Never walk away from the plate after a strikeout, blaming the umpire or acting upset. It's part of the game and umpires will make terrible calls from time to time. Don't let them see you upset or maybe your next AB ends the same way. Although this book is not intended to teach mechanics, I do want to mention something. Please don't get caught up in today's talk about exit velocity and launch angles. I have seen this result in young kids swinging for the fences with an extreme uppercut swing. No good. Any good hitting coach will tell you that the angle of your swing should match the same plain or angle that the pitch is traveling. It's referred to as keeping your bat in the zone as long as possible. This will result in a better percentage of making good contact with the ball. As far as exit velocity, that comes with good mechanics and getting stronger.

CHAPTER 11

BASE RUNNING

Being on base is a great feeling; whether you got there because of a hit or walk, you're on base with a chance to help your team score. You must be a smart baserunner. First, pay close attention to your base coaches. Do not look at where the ball is hit, and admire your work. Run to the base you're heading to and look at the coach for a sign to keep running or stop at that base. He may also give you signs to hit the base standing up or sliding. A common mistake young players make is not knowing how to run the bases properly. On a ball hit in the infield, it will be a race between you and the fielder playing the ball to get to first base. Unfortunately, you are racing a thrown baseball, which can travel much faster than you can run. The coach will tell you to run through the bag at first base because it is the only chance you will have of beating the throw. First base is also the only base you are allowed to overrun. When you do run through and past the first base bag, you must turn into foul territory. If you turn toward fair territory, you can be tagged out, as that will look like an attempt to go to second base.

I can't stress this part enough about running the bases, RUN every single time you hit the ball. There are no automatic outs, and everyone can make a mistake in the field that may help you reach a base safely. I don't care if you hit a ground ball right to a player in the infield or a pop up that looks easy.

It's crucial to run out every play. I've witnessed instances where routine fly balls to the outfield turned into triples because the outfielder misplayed them, allowing the ball to go over their head. Had the batter given up and not run, they might have ended up with just a single or, worse, thrown out at first from the outfield. Even foul balls should be run out until the umpire calls foul. When hitting a ball to the outfield that isn't caught, reaching first base is highly probable. In such cases, you should run to first with the intention of rounding the base and appearing ready to head for second. *'Cutting the bases'* refers to adjusting your base path based on the coach's signal; for instance, if your coach signals you to head for second while approaching first base, you should be able to see the signal early enough to adjust your route slightly.

You need to go a little bit into foul territory and cut in towards first base in the direction of second base. Without cutting the base, your momentum will take you too far toward the outfield and not second base. That longer route will give the fielder more time to get you out at second. Remember, the ball is traveling much faster than you can run. You need to try and create a path as straight to the bag as you can. The coach will always tell you to make a hard turn at first base towards second on balls hit to the outfield. They may say to hold up at first and see how quickly you must get back to touch the bag. They may also be waving you to go to second.

If you see the wave, then you must start your cut towards second and not slow down. As soon as you are headed to second, you need to look immediately over to your third base coach and see if they want you to keep running or stop at second. If they wave you over to keep running, start your cut around second as well keeping as straight a line as you can going to third. They will then start giving you the sign for what to do next as you approach third base. Pay close attention to whether or not the third base coach is telling you to slide at a base. This means the play will be close, and by sliding, you have a better chance of reaching the base safely. Too many times, kids don't slide and get tagged out. This happens because the runner must slow down to tag the base.

Remember, you cannot overrun second or third base. By sliding, you don't have to slow down; the ground does that for you. You will also be lower to the ground, which makes the tag harder for the fielder to make. You will see runners being called safe many times because they were able to slide under a tag attempt.

Baseball awareness plays a huge part in base running. You need to know the score, the outs, the pitch count, and the sign the batter is getting from the coach. Sometimes, you see a "hit and run" call, which means you are stealing on the pitch, and the batter is swinging the bat. There are no guarantees the batter will get a good pitch to swing at or that he will hit the ball at all. You need to recognize the pitchers' skills as well as the catcher's skills. If you are really paying attention to the game, you will notice the other players on the field and the skills they may have-which outfielders have a strong arm, are they accurate with their throws, and can they track a ball?

Tagging up is another situation you may find yourself in. If a ball is hit in the air to the outfield and there are less than two outs, you may be able to advance to the next base or even score after the ball is caught. The timing means everything when tagging up. You must wait until the ball is in the fielder's glove before your foot comes off the base you are on. If you are caught leaving early and the fielder throws the ball to the base you were on, you can be called out.

The pitcher also has the option to appeal a tag up if he thinks the runner may have left early. In that situation, it looks like the play is over, and the pitcher gets ready to throw a pitch to the next batter but instead throws over to the base the runner was on. The fielder tags the base, and the umpire makes the call, out or safe. When tagging up, please listen to your coach.

Your focus as the runner should be the base you are running to after the catch. The coach will tell you when to go. All this knowledge and awareness make you a better base runner who makes better decisions on the basepaths.

There are countless base running scenarios, so I can't go through them all, but one important thing to remember, if you remember anything, is to watch and listen to your base coaches while on or running the bases and not the parents or fans.

CHAPTER 12

STEALING BASES

When you're a baserunner, your job is to have the pitcher and catcher thinking about you and not just the batter. If you are not taking a big enough lead off the base, the pitcher and catcher are not worried about you because they know the catcher will have enough time to throw you out. A rule of thumb for leading is to go far enough that it takes you one step and a dive back to the base. If a pitcher makes a pickoff attempt and you simply step or walk back to first, you are not taking a big enough lead, and they aren't worried about you.

As a matter of fact, a good way to judge if you are far enough is whether or not the pitcher even bothers to throw over. If they throw over a lot, they are worried about you, and that distracts them from pitching their best to the batter. There are two stages to your lead from any base. The primary lead that we just mentioned is where you are positioned far enough for a one-step and dive back to the base, and your secondary lead comes on the delivery of the pitch. This lead is an aggressive few more steps further than the primary lead because the ball is thrown to the catcher, and they have a much further throw to try and pick you off.

Remember that catchers usually have strong arms, and if you are not paying attention, they can throw a quick snap throw, back to the base you are leading from and get you out. When you do have to get back to a base on a pickoff attempt, you want to make sure you are diving back to the left side of the base. This will make the receiver of the ball have to reach further for you to tag you out. Also, make sure you turn your head away from the throw so as not to get hit in the face by the ball or by the receiver's glove.

Timing on steal attempts makes all the difference between being successful or getting thrown out. It can be tough to steal off a pitcher with a good pickoff move, but if you know what to look for, you can be successful. The pitcher will be pitching from a stretch position rather than a full windup. Good pitchers will develop a good slide step which means no leg kick. These techniques of pitching allow for the ball to get to the catcher more quickly, so they have the time they need to throw you out. A good runner will watch the feet of the pitcher. Here comes another rule of thumb - for righty pitchers, if their front foot moves first, you're going to steal.

If their back foot moves first, they are possibly throwing over to try and pick you off. Some pitchers at higher levels can fool even the best baserunners with their footwork, but again, it's just a basic rule of thumb for getting a good jump to steal. Trying to steal second base off a lefty pitcher is even tougher. This is because they are facing directly at the runner on first and do not have to step off the rubber before throwing it over. Instead, they must step towards first instead of home plate when attempting a pickoff. This move can be sudden or a tricky move that looks like a normal leg kick but instead of the pitcher making the first move towards home, they step towards first. Stealing second is much more common than stealing third because of the far throw the catcher must make to second.

Stealing third is rare, especially at the pro level. At younger ages the thing to be more aware of when you are on base is passed balls and wild pitches. I see kids giving up their secondary leads way too early. Take an aggressive secondary lead, but don't rush back to the base, assuming the catcher will catch every pitch. If they miss a pitch and you are leaning back towards the base you came from, you miss your shot to steal a base. If you wait to be sure the catcher makes a clean catch, you give yourself a good chance to take the next base much more easily if they don't. Above all, pay attention to your coaches. There is nothing worse than missing signs on the basepaths. There is no sign for stealing on a passed ball. Most of the time, you're stealing unless you're playing on a field with a very close backstop. Again, take directions from your coach.

Chapter 13

College Recruitment

When I refer to colleges, I also include universities. There is a misconception out there that says, if you are good they will find you. Good luck with that. Even if you are a household name in your area, the only colleges that may hear about you will be local colleges. You must get out there and be seen. This is a very touchy subject, and some travel organizations may not agree with me, but it is not the travel team you are on that will get you looks from colleges. It's the experience you have when they see you play. You can spend the big money on the more well-known travel teams who usually end up with the better players, or you can be on an inexpensive town team.

The teams with the best players will win more trophies and get more social media exposure and therefore, get more business. Yes, I said business. It's a very good business, too. Roughly $4,000 for a kid to play on a travel team, not counting the travel expenses of hotels and food. What you will get for that money is the coaching. These organizations will pay coaches with at least college-level experience to coach your kids. This is a good thing. Your kid will learn fundamental baseball skills as well as hear stories about what it takes to play baseball in college. So, I would say by the age of

13, you should be looking to be on a travel team with good coaching.

It doesn't have to be the $4,000 team that wins every tournament. It can be a town team or a more inexpensive team, but the one ingredient they will need no matter where they play is playing time. I would always look for the teams that had the best coaches for my kids. It didn't have to be the best team. Just the team where I thought my kids were getting the best coaching for the money. I would rather they play on a team than sit on the bench because there are too many players for the same positions. The other ingredient is hard work. No matter what team they play on, they need to put the work in on their own to be college-ready.

Private lessons are a must, especially for pitcher and hitters. The mechanics of pitching and hitting are so important. They can help reduce injury number one but are essential to be even looked at by a college coach. College scouts have the knowledge and experience to see talent as well as projected talent. That comes from seeing mechanics and knowing what they are looking at. People may say that you can't teach speed. I say you have natural talent and speed, but I have seen both of my kids throw harder and run faster just by improving their mechanics and strength training. Same with hitting.

Unfortunately, in today's world, everyone is looking at radar guns to evaluate baseball. How fast can you pitch, how fast can you throw a baseball from the infield or outfield, and how fast is the ball coming off your bat? One of the reasons why college coaches look at these numbers is projectability. There are different levels of college baseball, but I will only focus on the ones that I have researched trying to help my son decide. That would be D1, D2, D3, and JUCO (Junior College).

In my experience and from what I have seen with other kids, you must get yourself out there to be seen. The best way is to make a list of all the colleges that have the field of study you want. Then, look at where they are located, what type of campus, big or small, the tuition, and lastly, the baseball program. Be realistic of your playing level. Once you have those, narrow it down to 10. Start putting together your baseball resume. Your resume should be both written and some videos of what you do best. Go to the college website and start sending emails to the head coach, assistant coaches, and, if you pitch, the pitching coach.

Let them know your academic stats, such as GPA and any honors or clubs you may belong to. Let them know why you are interested in their school specifically and tell them about yourself and why you would be a good fit at their school. Show how you play in games as well as training sessions. Do NOT make the videos long. No coach will sit through a 10-pitch at bat to watch you hit a single. Send 1-minute clips of the actual hit or, if you pitch, a strikeout. Not all the batters you faced in an inning.

Short videos where they can see your mechanics and your composure. Send them metrics numbers for pitching or throwing speeds, running speeds, and batting stats for a recent season. Invite them to see you at a game or a showcase that you will be playing.

If they respond that they will attend, tell your travel and/or high school coaches so they can help you prepare and make sure you are in that game. You must get in front of coaches to be recruited. In your email, ask if they will be attending any showcases that you can get to.

Numerous online recruiting sites offer services where you can pay to access college information and discover which showcases they will attend. However, it's essential to be cautious because these sites won't guarantee recruitment, and you'll still need to do most of the legwork yourself. They can also be quite expensive, and in my opinion, you can achieve similar results without them. Once you sign up, you'll likely start receiving numerous camp and showcase invitations. While this might make you feel valued and important, it's important to maintain a level-headed approach and recognize that these invitations don't necessarily guarantee genuine interest from coaches.

Coaches often need to raise funds for their teams, which they often do through hosting camps and showcases. However, be wary of expensive showcases that promise recruitment for a hefty fee. Instead, focus on attending individual college camps at campuses you're interested in. These camps offer the advantage of being seen exclusively by the coaching staff of that particular college. While you may still need to pay to attend these camps, the costs are typically lower.

Additionally, consider participating in affordable showcases where you can obtain official metric numbers to send to coaches. It's crucial to note that all communication with colleges should come directly from the player, not their parents. Coaches want to assess the communication skills and personalities of prospective players and prefer to interact directly with them as young adults. While parents should be involved in decision-making, initial discussions with college coaches should be led by the player.

CHAPTER 14

COLLEGE DIVISION LEVELS

D1- What I found with D1 level college for baseball is that you must be a very good academic student because they focus so much on baseball. Your level of play must be considered above average. They want kids who are not only good at baseball but who are less likely to struggle with grades. The acceptance GPA may be high even without baseball, typically between 3.5 and 4.0.

Remember, you can be a great player and have a D1 interest, but you still must get accepted by the college. There are more scholarship opportunities at D1. Due to the high GPA score, you can get a lot of the tuition cost knocked down, and you can get more money for sports with D1. Having a high SAT or ACT score can help, but submitting low scores can hurt. Some colleges today leave the SAT or ACT scores optional. You must inquire with each school you apply to. The worst thing to happen to both players and coaches is to have a great player fail academically which would disqualify them from playing and losing their scholarship. This is true at any level, but there is less time to focus on grades at D1 if you tend to struggle.

The team will be traveling a lot during the baseball season. When they are on the road, it is up to the student to keep up with classwork on their own. That can be very difficult for some students. The team can travel far distances for about 6 weeks or so before returning to play closer to home again for the rest of the season. The student is still responsible for all the schoolwork.

D2 – D2 is still at a very high level of baseball. The main difference besides skill level is the focus on academics. D2 is more evenly split. They focus a lot of time on baseball and training but give equal time to keep grades up. You don't need a high GPA from high school to be accepted, but it cannot be too low either. Typically, your GPA should be between 2.7 and 3.5 or higher. The higher your GPA, the more academic money you may receive toward tuition. D2 colleges do not get as many scholarship opportunities as D1, and there is very little money available for baseball. It is mostly through academics you will receive the scholarships. And, of course, the better-recruited players will get better offers. D2 teams also travel a lot, so you still need to be on top of your studies when you're on the road. You also need to have good relationships with your professors because they know what the demands are when you miss class for sports. You want their support and help if needed.

D3 – With D3, there is more of a focus on academics, and they offer no sports scholarship money. Many kids decide to go D3 even if they have the skill to play higher. This is because they know what field of study they want in college and many of the top colleges and universities in the country are D3. You can be accepted with a lower GPA, but many kids with GPAs as high as

4.0 choose D3 because they know what they are looking for with education. As with all levels, D3 colleges have strict requirements to fulfill your academic requirements, but they offer a lot of help to achieve them. Don't get me wrong, D1 and D2 offer plenty of help but there is also a high focus on the sport. Typically, D3 teams don't travel for as long a period as D1 or D2. They usually only travel during spring break, so no classes are missed.

JUCO – Junior College is a great option for a few reasons. One reason is you may be looking to get your master's degree in a particular field. So, you do two years at one school, and you get to play baseball at the same time. Then, try to move to a four-year school to finish, where you may still be able to play baseball. Another reason is maybe you struggled with academics in high school, but you are an advanced ballplayer. You can go to a JUCO school to work on your academics and then transfer to a D1, D2, or D3 school. Lastly, maybe you're a good academic student but need more time to develop your baseball skills.

The difference in playing time is a big factor in choosing the right school as well. Many kids want to play right away in their freshman year and not wait until their sophomore or even junior year to play. Let's face it, the best players will play at whatever level you are on. The best D1 players will play on the D1 teams. If you don't play or think you should be playing, look for D2. Many D1-level players who might be considered second-string players will drop a level to D2 where now they will be the starters. The D2 kids who thought they were good enough to start may now have to wait or drop a level themselves to D3 to play. I'm sorry if this doesn't sound very encouraging, but the bottom line is college coaches get paid to win baseball games, not make sure everyone gets in the game like it was in Little League.

Pitchers have the best chance of playing at every level because most teams will carry at least 13 pitchers. Some carry more. Catchers are the next top recruited position. You need a few good quality catchers especially because of how demanding the position is and how the players are prone to injury. The big difference is catchers must also hit very well whereas most pitchers won't get to hit. To earn a starting position player spot, you must be especially good because there are only 7 positions on the field after pitchers and catchers. The team will typically carry 30 or more position players.

That's roughly 4 or 5 players at each position. Now, remember I said most kids at the D1 and D2 levels will have to wait until their sophomore or even junior year to play. So, many of the team members will be up-and-coming freshmen who will be developing the skills they need to compete at the college level. This is not a bad thing. The real purpose of going to college in the first place is to get a higher education for a possible career you are interested in. So, the opportunity to play baseball and have some money towards tuition is not a bad deal.

Make the most of it. For the most part, if you get recruited as a pitcher, you will only pitch. Yes, there are always exceptions to every rule. There are unique players who can pitch well but are also good hitters. Now, that's not to say that there are not a lot of pitchers who can do both, but teams don't look for that. There are very specific workouts for pitchers and special workouts for position players. It is extremely difficult to do both.

If you are a good pitcher, the coach may not want to risk you getting hurt while at bat or running bases. Like I said before, there are a few players for every position. You would have to be an exceptional hitter to do both and take someone else out of the lineup. There have only been two MLB players in history to do it, Babe Ruth and Shoei Ohtani. I understand that in Little League, the best athletes are usually the kids who pitch, play shortstop, and bat in the top four in the lineup. As they get older, that changes, and usually, by the time they hit high school, they excel at one or the other. Even if they still can do both very well in high school, that doesn't mean they will do both in college.

You would have the best chance of being a two-way player at the D3 level or JUCO. That is another reason why some really good players choose to play at those levels. If a kid is a junior in high school and he can already pitch 90 mph, well, his projectability is very high, and he will have D1-level colleges very interested in them. They know that with growth, training, and a few mechanical tweaks, they could be throwing 95 by their sophomore or junior year in college. That doesn't mean that you must throw 90 to be considered for D1. It just means you have a head start. A kid can be throwing 85 and still get D1 looks if their ball has movement, and if they have very good control of their pitches. D2 pitchers are usually throwing 80 to 88 mph by their junior year in high school.

Again, pitch command and ball movement help. D3 and JUCO pitchers can be in the high 70's to 85 mph and be successful. You will have pitchers who throw faster than their level because they drop down a level to play more. Academics play a very important role in the level you will get accepted to. There are some good ballplayers who may have struggled with their grades in high school, so they go to a JUCO to improve their grades and maybe transfer after. Those players may be D1-level players.

Some say if you want to have a shot at playing professional baseball, you must play D1 in college. Not true. You must be seen, and if you are seen with the right stuff, you will get your chance. Many kids from D2, D3, and JUCO get their chance. You may have to put in more of the work because it may be true that pro scouts do not attend as many games as they do at the D1 level. But if you have what it takes, then make every effort to be seen. College coaches can help you find out about pro scout camps and showcases.

Believe me, pro scouts are looking and paying attention. One thing I want to stress is the odds of making it to the MLB. I heard someone say once that you have a better chance of getting hit by lightning while standing in line to cash your winning lottery ticket than being drafted into the MLB. I hope that's not true because that statement is very discouraging. When I was trying to explain to my kids what those odds meant, they gave me a great response. They said, "You have less of a chance of getting struck by lightning if you stay inside and do nothing, and you have zero chance of winning the lottery if you don't play." If there is still a chance, as small as it may be, there is a chance. If you play the lottery every day and go outside in every storm, your chances go up. Not that anyone should be playing out in storms hoping to be struck by lightning. It's just a figure of speech.

The point is, if you work hard every day and get out there to be seen, you have a shot. Looking at those odds, you still need to have a career plan in place while you work on your dream. You do not want to be in a spot where you put everything into that small chance, and if it doesn't happen, you have nowhere to go. I know so many kids who played baseball at a high level and went on to play in college. If they didn't get that call by the time college was over, they went on to find a career with the degree they worked so hard to get. I will finish this chapter by saying if you want something you must work hard to achieve it. Don't put all your eggs in one basket. Go to college to be a student first and an athlete second. If you are good enough to play after college, that would be awesome, but make sure you have a good plan for your career after baseball.

CHAPTER 15

LIFE

I said at the beginning of this book that I could compare any life situation to a baseball situation. Not knowing all your life situations, I can only mention what I think is important at this time. The first thing I say about life and baseball is the fact that you need to have people in your life that you can depend on. In baseball, it is obvious that you need to be able to depend on your coaches and teammates. Your coaches guide you, and your teammates support you. In life, those people may be family, friends, co-workers, religious groups, and so on.

You start life getting guidance from your parents and support from your family and friends. It is so important to have the right people in your life to help you through tough times as well as celebrate your achievements. Your teammates will help prepare you for a life of working together to get a job done. You will need this skill in your career. You need to know how to follow directions in baseball as well as in life. You need to understand rules, boundaries, and consequences. Baseball and life have them both.

Be competitive with other teams, not with your teammates. Be competitive with other companies and not your co-workers. Remember, you may see and pass the same people while you're climbing the ladder of success that you may see on your way down.

People remember how you treated them. To be successful in the game of baseball, you must prepare. I said earlier that I tell my students, you can't just show up to practices and games and expect to be at their best. That same philosophy applies to your career.

Simply showing up to school or work isn't enough to excel in your career. To reach the top of your field, you must invest your own time in learning as much as possible about your industry. Just like in baseball, where players on the bench need to be prepared to enter the game at any moment, you must also be ready to step into new roles or positions. This means understanding the responsibilities and challenges associated with the position you aspire to or are being considered for. In baseball, as in life, failure is inevitable, but it's how we learn and grow from those failures that ultimately determines our success.

You are considered a great hitter if you get out 7 out of 10 times. Yes, I said 7 out of 10 times you don't get a hit you are great. That means that you only get a hit 3 out of 10 times. J.K Rowlings, who wrote the Harry Potter books, was rejected at least 12 times before the book was published. Look at her now. She never gave up. In baseball, you have a game where you may get four at-bats. Four chances to get a hit. Maybe you get out all four times.

Guess what? You get another four chances in the next game. Then you get another four chances in the game after that, and the next, and so on. An average season for a travel team is about thirty games. That's about 120 potential at-bats. That's one season. If you play travel baseball from the ages of 10 to 17, then that's over 800 at-bats. I didn't even count school ball, which could double those numbers. I also didn't mention that you have at least 3 pitches to swing at with each at-bat. The point is you get many chances to do your job as a hitter. To be successful, you must be able to see the times you failed and what you can do to help you succeed the next time.

In your career, you will fail and make mistakes. You must be able to recognize those mistakes and make corrections. Unfortunately, failing 7 out of 10 times in your career is not a good thing. Learn from the mistakes you make. I once had a kid challenge me by asking me how his situation in life could relate to baseball. He told me his father had to take another job and couldn't attend as many games to watch him play. Of course, this made him sad. I reminded him of a sacrifice bunt.

You know you will most likely get out, but it will also help the team in the long run. I told him his father was making sacrifices to help his family. Yes, he misses more games, and that will make him sad, too, but he knows the extra money will help the family in the long run.

Another player told me that their best friend moved away, and they were very upset. He asked, *"How can you compare this to a baseball situation?"* Well, if you watch the big leaguers who have been on a team for a long time, become friends with their teammates, and suddenly get traded, they must adjust. They may not be able to replace the friends they made or ever be as close as they were with their former teammates, but they do make new friends and create new bonds on their new team. You miss your friends and teammates but need to look ahead and know that if you bring your strengths to the team, you will both be successful. Relationships are similar in that you may not see someone you cared about as often but you can and will meet new friends so that you can be happy again. Having the right attitude in baseball and life is extremely important.

Be positive, remember who you are and your strengths and work on your weaknesses. If you get up to bat and think about how fast the pitcher is throwing and that he struck you out last inning, chances are he will strike you out again. If you think about how he struck you out and learned from it, you have a better chance of getting a hit. Maybe you must swing earlier or adjust your approach. It's the same in life.

Try not to think about failures as failures. Think of them as learning experiences you will have a different approach to next time. Think about the times when things worked right, and you hit the ball out of the park. Pun intended. There will be times in life when you will be the hero and times when you feel like you let people down. It's the same in baseball. Learn from the bad times and remember when you were the hero.

Remember that it is ok to ask for help when needed and that the people who love you want to be there for you. It makes people feel good when they know they made a difference. Treat people the way you want to be treated. Have good sportsmanship. Don't be a sore loser. Don't be a bad winner. Say thank you and please. Remember times that were tough, and remember how you got through them. Look positively at any new task. With hard work, you will succeed. Be the person or teammate that you would want to be around.

Teach others the things that you have learned. Above all, enjoy your life to the fullest. Get out there and try new things. Don't be afraid to fail, or rather, don't be afraid to learn. This is true in life and in any sport you may play.

There are three levels of people who will be successful. A 3rd rate player will rely on natural talent and hope it is enough. They may think they are strong enough, big enough, or smart enough and not put the work in. A 2nd rate player will go with the flow. They study if everyone else is studying. They work out if everyone else is working out. A 1st rate player doesn't wait for anyone. They study on their own, they work out on their own. They are doing these things for themselves to be the best that they can be.

Remember bringing your best to any situation, life or sports, makes you a great team player. I wish you nothing but the best in the great game of baseball and, most of all, life.

Made in the USA
Monee, IL
05 October 2024

9d28bf38-f422-4e48-88ac-e4b53c5f6d64R01